Commando Operations

Other Publications:

HOW THINGS WORK
WINGS OF WAR
CREATIVE EVERYDAY COOKING
COLLECTOR'S LIBRARY OF THE UNKNOWN
CLASSICS OF WORLD WAR II
TIME-LIFE LIBRARY OF CURIOUS AND UNUSUAL FACTS
AMERICAN COUNTRY
VOYAGE THROUGH THE UNIVERSE
THE THIRD REICH
THE TIME-LIFE GARDENER'S GUIDE
MYSTERIES OF THE UNKNOWN
TIME FRAME
FIX IT YOURSELF
FITNESS, HEALTH & NUTRITION
SUCCESSFUL PARENTING
HEALTHY HOME COOKING
UNDERSTANDING COMPUTERS
LIBRARY OF NATIONS
THE ENCHANTED WORLD
THE KODAK LIBRARY OF CREATIVE PHOTOGRAPHY
GREAT MEALS IN MINUTES
THE CIVIL WAR
PLANET EARTH
COLLECTOR'S LIBRARY OF THE CIVIL WAR
THE EPIC OF FLIGHT
THE GOOD COOK
WORLD WAR II
HOME REPAIR AND IMPROVEMENT
THE OLD WEST

For information on and a full description of any
of the Time-Life Books series listed above,
please call 1-800-621-7026 or write:
Reader Information
Time-Life Customer Service
P.O. Box C-32068
Richmond, Virginia 23261-2068

THE NEW FACE OF WAR

Commando Operations

BY THE EDITORS OF
TIME-LIFE BOOKS, ALEXANDRIA, VIRGINIA

CONSULTANTS

CALEB BAKER is the land warfare correspondent for *Defense News*. He is an authority on special operations, helicopters, unmanned aerial vehicles, chemical warfare, Asia, and Central America.

THOMAS DONNELLY, a former deputy editor and land warfare correspondent of *Defense News*, has been editor of *Army Times* since 1987.

COMMANDER ANTHONY M. FRANZITTA, retired from the U.S. Navy, served on a number of fast attack and ballistic missile class submarines. He has also served as a submarine tactics instructor at the U.S. Naval Submarine School and as a battle group antisubmarine warfare instructor at the Atlantic Fleet Tactical Training Group.

ROY HOLMES, the manager for image intensification systems development at ITT's Electro-Optical Products Division in Roanoke, Virginia, has been developing night-vision equipment since 1985.

COLONEL RODERICK J. LENAHAN (Ret.) served as the senior intelligence officer for the Iranian Rescue Task Force, retiring in July 1988 as chief of intelligence for the Air Force Special Operations Command.

THOMAS S. LOGSDON has been an engineer and systems analyst since 1964 at Rockwell International, where he performed advanced systems studies for the Navstar Global Positioning System. He writes and lectures on computer technology and robotics, among other topics.

CAPTAIN HUGH McMANNERS fought with the Special Boat Squadron in the Falklands War; as a captain, he commanded the squadron's artillery and naval gunfire forward observation team.

DAVID L. MAGNONE, retired from the U.S. Navy, is a veteran of special operations in Vietnam, the Middle East, and the Pacific Rim. He specializes in communications and electro-optics and was officer in charge of a Naval Special Warfare Special Operations communications unit.

MARGARET ROTH, an editor for *Army Times*, *Navy Times*, and *Air Force Times*, has written extensively about Panama-United States relations and Operation Just Cause.

COLONEL T. C. SKANCHY, recently retired from the U.S. Air Force, commanded a fighter wing and the F-15 Division, Fighter Weapons School at Nellis Air Force Base, Nevada. He also served there as the vice commander of Red Flag, the Air Force's combined air operations training program.

SERGEANT FIRST CLASS MICHAEL SMITH, a former Delta Force member, participated in Operation Urgent Fury in Grenada in 1983. Smith was part of the assault team assigned to strike the Richmond Hill Prison.

COMMANDER GARY L. STUBBLEFIELD, retired from the U.S. Navy, served more than twenty years as a Navy SEAL. He led operations in Vietnam, Central America, and the Persian Gulf and commanded both SEAL Team Three and Special Boat Squadron One.

MAJOR GENERAL JULIAN THOMPSON commanded Three Commando Brigade during the Falklands War. He is now senior research fellow at the department of war studies, King's College, London.

BRICE VICAN was part of the Second Battalion, 75th Ranger Regiment, which parachuted onto Grenada during Operation Urgent Fury in 1983.

CONTENTS

Pound for Pound, None Finer

Before the Persian Gulf War, General Norman Schwarzkopf, like most soldiers in the regular military, had little use for special-operations forces. They looked great in the movies, he thought, but in a real war, they would just get in the way.

As Desert Shield turned to Desert Storm, however, necessity changed this view. And by war's end, the 9,400 special-ops personnel deployed to the Gulf—members of the Army's Rangers, Green Berets, and Delta Force; Navy sea-air-land teams (SEALs); and Air Force special-ops squadrons, as well as a handful of men from Britain's Special Air Service (SAS) and Special Boat Squadron (SBS)—had earned his praise.

They did so by performing valuable, dangerous, and highly secret missions across the breadth of Iraq and occupied Kuwait. To open the war, U.S. Air Force special-operations choppers led a team of Army Apache attack helicopters on a successful mission to destroy crucial Iraqi early-warning radar sites. Earlier, a team of Delta Force and SAS troopers captured a complete SA-8 surface-to-air missile system and helicoptered it to Saudi Arabia for analysis before coalition pilots took to the sky.

Three Green Berets infiltrated within 100 miles of Baghdad to report on road traffic into Kuwait. Found hiding by a little girl, they ensured a fight by not shooting her with silenced 9-mm pistols. ("We couldn't live with ourselves," said one of the trio later.) They held off 100 Iraqi infantrymen until extracted in the nick of time by a special-ops helicopter.

On another mission, American and British teams in western Iraq found twenty-six Scud missiles poised for barrage attack on Israel. Calling in an air strike, the commandos shone beams of invisible laser light on the missiles as A-10 Thunderbolt jets dropped laser-guided bombs, shattering the Scuds before they could be launched. In a private message, Schwarzkopf later wrote: "You guys kept Israel out of the war."

Troopers of the Army's 17th Cavalry Regiment push an OH-58D observation helicopter to a hangar on the destroyer O'Brien. Playing a special-ops role, the unit flew nighttime reconnaissance over the Persian Gulf.

Marine special-ops troops in Saudi Arabia launch a kayak. Such boats were used during the Gulf War to conduct beach reconnaissance near Kuwait City.

Navy SEALs in Saudi Arabia waterproof the weapons and electronics gear they will carry in inflatable boats on a night mission off the Kuwaiti coast.

The Air Force was well represented in Gulf War special operations. At left, an airman fast-ropes from an MH-53J Pave Low helicopter; below, a communications specialist erects a portable satellite antenna.

SEALs board Pave Low helicopters at a sand-swept Marine Corps landing zone in northern Saudi Arabia. The site was so remote that the troops named it Lonesome Dove.

This 15,000-pound bomb, bearing a message to the Iraqis, was dropped from a special-operations MC-130H transport to spur Iraqis to surrender.

In anticipation of house-to-house fighting to liberate Kuwait City, Green Berets of the Fifth Special Forces Group practice rappelling with the Kuwaiti special-operations troops they would accompany into the capital.

Debris from an Iraqi bunker, blown sky-high by Army Rangers during the ground war, rains down over an abandoned tank, which the so-called Bunker Busters also destroyed after the dust settled.

Soon after the liberation of Kuwait City, two members of the Third Special Forces Group search for snipers outside the American embassy.

Three SEALs—a gunner (top), driver, and navigator—patrol Kuwait City in a $50,000 fast-attack vehicle. A 40-mm automatic grenade launcher sits in front of the gunner, AT-4 antitank missile launchers to either side.

One Night's Work in the Persian Gulf

Covered by their mates aboard a U.S. Navy landing craft, two SEALs board the *Iran Ajr* at dawn on September 22, 1987. The vessel had been surprised the night before laying mines in the Persian Gulf.

Night. It was their element. In it, they had been trained to see, to fight, and to kill. It served as the motif for their nickname—the Night Stalkers—and their chilling motto: Death waits in the dark. Now, late on September 21, 1987, the helicopter commandos of the Army's mysterious 160th Aviation Group, better known as Task Force 160, stood poised for action on the deck of the guided-missile frigate *Jarrett*, sailing the troubled waters of the Persian Gulf thirty miles northeast of the island nation of Bahrain.

Their quarry was the *Iran Ajr*, an old Iranian Navy landing craft that American intelligence had learned was serving as a minelayer. Iranian leaders steadfastly denied that they were mining the Gulf, but there could be no question about the ship's purpose. Infrared photographs of the vessel taken by the crew of a Navy P-3 Orion patrol plane clearly revealed the crew pushing spiked globes overboard. They could only be mines. Nor could there be any question as to the *Ajr*'s position. In addition to the P-3, an American KH-11 satellite and Air Force SR-71 Blackbird high-altitude photoreconnaissance jets had been monitoring the voyage of the 157-foot *Ajr* for three days.

Mines posed a considerable threat to shipping in the Gulf. In July, a Kuwaiti oil tanker, under U.S. Navy escort to thwart attacks promised by the Iranians, had its hull ripped open by one of the devices. Floating mines spotted by shipboard lookouts had been detonated by rifle fire. Other mines were neutralized by huge Navy helicopters towing minesweeping sleds across the water's surface. Washington suspected that the Iranians were to blame for the infestation but could not prove the charge or retaliate without catching them in the act.

To gain such evidence, Admiral William J. Crowe, Jr., chairman of the Joint Chiefs of Staff, turned to the Night Stalkers. Visiting Rear Admiral Harold Bernsen, commander of the American Middle East Force, aboard his flagship, the USS *La Salle*, early in September, Crowe ordered TF 160 to sneak up on an Iranian ship while it was laying mines and disable it. Then Navy SEALs from the USS *Guadalcanal* were to board the vessel, seizing it as evidence against Iran. Bernsen was put in charge of the operation, and participating personnel from all the services, including Task Force 160, were placed under his command.

Volunteers all, the Night Stalkers were likely candidates to gain the propaganda victory that Washington so desperately wanted.

The unit had been formed in October 1981, eighteen months after eight U.S. servicemen died in an attempt to rescue fifty-three American diplomats and embassy staffers from captivity in Tehran. To the extent that the mission failed because of difficulties encountered flying helicopters long distances at night, U.S. officials became determined to avoid a similar calamity in the future. Special-operations helicopter units were formed, among them TF 160. Though conceived primarily as air support for special operations, Task Force 160 had the versatility, the training, and just the helicopter for Admiral Crowe's assignment—the compact, high-tech AH-6 attack chopper.

Also called the Little Bird, the highly maneuverable AH-6 is just twenty-four feet long and six feet wide. With its rotor blades folded back, it fits easily inside a truck having the dimensions of a moving van. Once on site, the helicopter can be readied for flight in minutes. And its compactness has another advantage: It renders the Little Bird hard to see by radar or with the naked eye. Further hindering detection are a high-speed, five-bladed main rotor and a four-bladed tail rotor that produce, instead of the loud, thumping noise characteristic of older rotors, a subdued whir. Depending on atmospheric conditions, an AH-6 at 500 feet can fly overhead without being heard, especially if there are other noises—the splashing of mines into the ocean, for example—to mask the sound of the helicopter. For fighting at night, when the helicopter is especially difficult to pinpoint, the Little Bird is equipped with a forward-looking infrared (FLIR) system. Armament includes 7.62-mm machine

During a training exercise, tracer rounds fired from the 7.62-mm machine guns of a low-flying AH-6 attack helicopter *(right)*—the same type used by Task Force 160 in the *Iran Ajr* raid—roil the water around a floating target *(left)*, then ricochet high into the sky.

guns, 2.75-inch rockets, and other weapons that, depending on the mission, can be mounted on fourteen-inch stubs extending from either side of the fuselage.

Task Force 160 pilots had trained meticulously with their equipment at Fort Campbell, Kentucky, their home base. They practiced only at night, often in violent storms, to master the art of high-speed, ground-hugging flight under appalling conditions. Sometimes they had only night-vision goggles and their instincts to guide them—an experience the pilots called "flying out on the edge." One exercise with night-vision goggles, intended to simulate a long-range insertion mission flown over water, involved skimming low over Lake Michigan for nearly ten hours. Such experience would soon prove valuable to the aviators aboard the *Jarrett*, who were biding their time under a moonless sky.

They did not have to wait long. When the *Iran Ajr* neared a point fifty miles northeast of the frigate, observers aboard a P-3 reported that the ship was again laying mines. Bernsen flashed an order to the 160th: Go have a look. In an instant, two Little Birds quietly lifted off the *Jarrett*'s deck. Flying 150 feet above the sea at fifty knots without lights, the AH-6s closed to within 500 yards of the gray Iranian vessel. Unheard by the crew, the Night Stalkers watched on their FLIR monitors. Aboard the *Ajr*, shadowy figures of sailors were doing precisely what had been suspected. At midnight, the pilot of the lead chopper radioed that the Iranians were "dropping objects overboard that appear to be mines." The crewmen, he said, were pushing them off a ten-foot gangplanklike platform.

Aboard the *La Salle*, Admiral Bernsen responded swiftly. At 12:03 a.m., the Little Birds received his curt one-word order: "Execute." Without warning, the helicopters opened up with a barrage from their 7.62-mm machine guns and sent several rockets slamming into the *Ajr*. A fuel drum toward the vessel's bow exploded, starting a fire. Another blaze erupted in the engine room.

The chopper pilots ceased firing and moved toward the *Ajr*, now dead in the water, for a closeup examination of the damage they had caused. Incredibly, sailors were still rushing about on deck, pushing more mines overboard. Pentagon analysts later guessed that the Iranians were trying to get rid of evidence. To stop them, at 12:41 a.m., Bernsen ordered the Night Stalkers to resume strafing. Once again, the Little Birds attacked the *Ajr*, this time setting the stern on fire. Then they returned to the *Jarrett*.

Members of a Navy explosive-ordnance-disposal team examine nine mines found on the *Iran Ajr*. All but two of the devices, which float beneath the surface of the water and explode when a passing ship strikes a protruding horn, were armed, mounted on wheels, and ready to be rolled overboard.

When the SEALs from the *Guadalcanal* boarded the crippled ship at dawn, they discovered just how effective the nighttime raids had been. The *Ajr* was a ghost ship. Three bodies had been left behind by fleeing crewmen. Windows were shattered. Huge gouges pocked the hull and cabin. And the Iranians had ransacked offices and other cabins in a hasty effort to destroy incriminating papers.

Navigating carefully to avoid hitting mines, the *Jarrett* found ten of the crewmen in rubber rafts and sixteen others, including four wounded sailors, either clinging to floating debris or swimming. The captain of the *Iran Ajr* was among the wounded. Delicately termed "detainees" instead of prisoners, the twenty-six Iranians were taken to the *La Salle*, and outfitted in jeans and souvenir shirts bearing the ship's name. Before being flown to Oman for release to the International Red Crescent, the Islamic version of the Red

Cross, the captain, besides telling of three of his crew who got away, helped find some of the mines that the *Iran Ajr* had planted.

Naval experts inspecting the ship found nine of the devices arrayed at mid-deck, all but two ready for use. They turned out to be the same type that had damaged the oil tanker in July. Recently manufactured in North Korea, they replicated a primitive Russian design dating from 1908. The *Iran Ajr* was later packed with explosives and scuttled.

The men of TF 160 who helped the United States earn this small but sweet victory do not call themselves commandos. Indeed, Great Britain's Royal Marines are one of the few forces in the world known officially by that name, and they are not considered members of the special-operations community. Yet when organizations such as the Army's

A Navy Sea Spectre patrol boat creeps toward a life raft containing an *Iran Ajr* crew member. He soon became one of twenty-six Iranians *(right)* taken captive in the hours after their vessel was seized. Intended for coastal patrol, the Sea Spectre is well armed: A Bofors 40-mm cannon commands the foredeck. Behind it is a .50-caliber machine gun *(pointed skyward)*, one of three on board. Aft of the wheelhouse stands a 20-mm gun.

Delta Force, Special Forces, and Rangers; the U.S. Air Force's First Special Operations Wing; and Britain's Special Air Service and Special Boat Squadron take the offensive as TF 160 and the SEALs did in capturing the *Iran Ajr*, the result is a commando action in anybody's book.

This so-called direct action in support of larger operations—the capture of the *Iran Ajr* took place in the context of conducting U.S.-flagged oil tankers safely through the hazards of the Persian Gulf—is only one of the many colors to be found on the special-operations palette. Much as they relish the lightning raid, such troops are just as likely to draw assignments ranging from surreptitious reconnaissance deep inside enemy-held territory—where the object often is to avoid contact with the enemy—and training soldiers of friendly nations. The U.S. Special Operations Command includes units that specialize in rebuilding the institutions of a war-ravaged society and others skilled in psychological operations (psyops) with the aim of demoralizing an enemy and persuading it not to fight.

Psychological operations also encompass deception. During the waning days of Operation Desert Shield, for example, special-operations troops, equipped with sound trucks blaring the sounds of helicopters and the rumble of tanks, faked the activity of an entire armored division. Meanwhile, the real armor moved west undetected to participate in the flanking action that defeated Iraqi forces in Kuwait and southern Iraq in February 1991. Shortly before that 100-hour ground war was to begin, SEALs in power boats motored toward the beach near Kuwait City, set explosives at the surf line, and strung buoys to mark the way for Marine landing craft—or so the enemy believed. In response to this and other frauds, Iraqi commanders moved two divisions toward the beach to repel an assault that never came.

While there can be no denying either the value or the risk of many exploits like these, more provocative are the missions in which small numbers of special-operations troops, often operating on the periphery of a large military undertaking, help prepare the way for the main force with advance raids against key installations, by seizing and securing airheads or beachheads for follow-on forces, and by generally pricking the enemy where least expected.

Such was the role of the Special Air Service and the Special Boat Squadron in 1982, during Britain's war to regain the Falkland Islands from Argentine invaders—and of American special-operations units in the actions taken to restore democratic government to Grenada in 1983 and Panama in 1989. For all these units, setbacks and defeats punctuated the successes. Some failures resulted from the conviction among these exquisitely trained men that almost no feat of arms is beyond them. Others can be traced to regular-force commanders who did not fully appreciate the merits—and limitations—of these special-purpose fighters.

The American experience in Grenada, where special-operations missions failed for one reason or another, showed that lack of co-ordination between the commando arms of various services can be fatal. Partly as a result of that ordeal, the Pentagon integrated all such forces into a single command. The benefits of doing so became evident in Panama, where the success rate of this kind of proceeding approached 100 percent. Achievements of special-operations forces in the Gulf War were even more substantial and at last may have raised the value of these troops in the eyes of conventional military commanders to something approaching their true worth.   ★

Special Delivery
by Submarine

Stealth is the stock in trade of special-operations forces. They conduct small-unit demolition raids, gather intelligence, or reconnoiter in advance of conventional troops; their success depends largely on not being discovered. Detection is most likely during insertion, and of all the ways to arrive for a mission, one of the riskiest is an approach from the sea. To minimize the chance of being seen by patrolling boats or aircraft, special-operations troops are frequently carried to their insertion points by submarine, a vessel that can move great distances secretly and fast.

The last couple of miles to shore are usually traveled by inflatable raiding craft stowed aboard the submarine. Circumstances determine how the men get into the boats. If the insertion point is screened from observation by the enemy and sea conditions permit, the submarine surfaces. Then the troops fill the raiding craft with air on deck and either lower them into the water for boarding or leave them on deck to float clear when the submarine dives.

When enemy patrols or shore-based radar makes surfacing unsafe for the submarine, the commandos launch their raiding craft underwater, as demonstrated by U.S. Navy SEALs on the following pages. Then, as the team starts its mission, the submarine slips away, unseen and unheard.

One hand for the boat. After exiting a submarine, a Navy SEAL grasps the forward escape hatch as the boat moves ahead at one or two knots to maintain depth.

An Intricate Exit

Before inflating their raiding craft and sending it to the surface *(page 26)*, SEALs must exit the submarine. The means for this maneuver is called an escape trunk. This special chamber, which is located forward of the sail on the fast attack submarine shown below, is open to the submarine interior through one hatch and to the sea through others. As illustrated at right, the escape trunk allows the divers to leave without flooding the submarine.

As many as five divers can fit in the chamber. Jammed together, the men must endure the close quarters for several minutes after they assemble in the escape trunk. This pause allows the men to adjust to the pressure of the seawater. At periscope depth of about 30 feet below the surface, sea pressure is approximately fifteen pounds per square inch, and acclimation takes about ten minutes. Raiding craft, however, can be launched from depths as great as 120 feet, where the divers must wait approximately fifteen minutes before leaving the escape trunk and getting on with the work of sending their gear to the surface. Rising to the surface from this depth takes an additional two minutes.

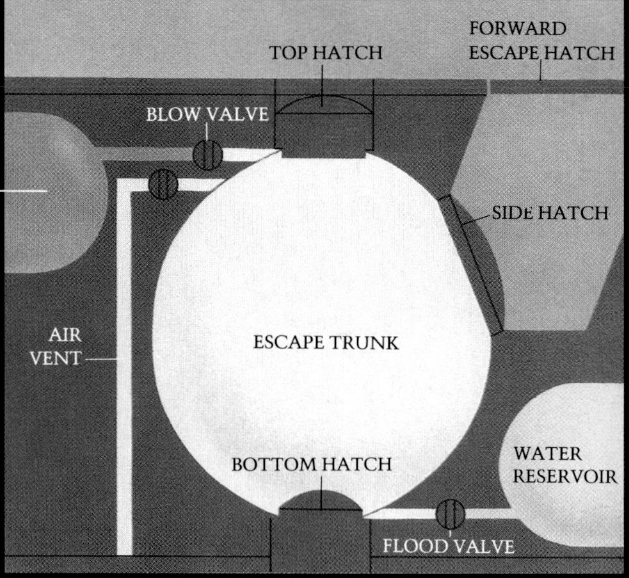

The escape trunk. Seawater stored aboard the sub, pressurized air, and simple valves are used to match inside and outside water pressure, allowing divers to pass safely through the side hatch. The top hatch is reserved for a deep-sea recovery capsule used to rescue the crew of a sunken submarine.

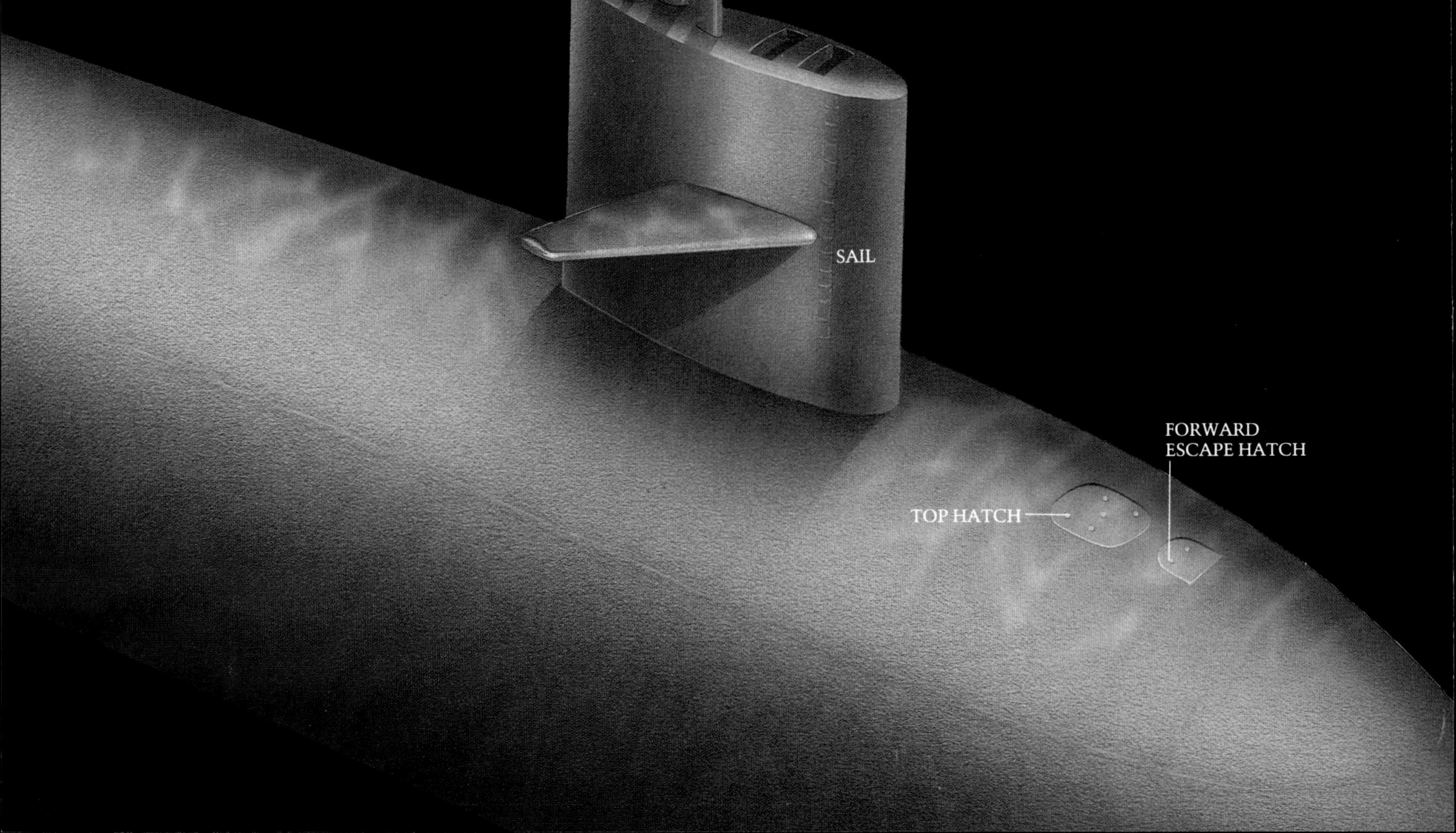

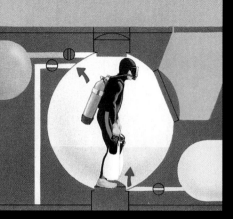

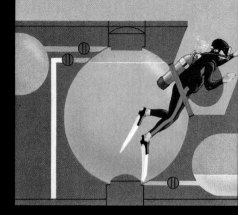

Flooding the chamber. A diver enters by way of the bottom hatch and seals it. Next, he opens the flood valve, letting water enter the chamber from a reservoir. (Adding water from outside the sub would change its buoyancy.) As air displaced by rising water escapes through a vent, the diver unlatches the side hatch, which sea pressure holds shut.

Stopping the flow. With the side hatch underwater, the swimmer closes the vent and the flood valve, then opens the blow valve. Doing so allows compressed air into the chamber, gradually raising the pressure inside the trunk.

Making an exit. When the pressures inside and outside the trunk are equal, the side hatch swings open. The diver closes the blow valve to prevent water and large air bubbles—which could betray the submarine's presence—from being forced through the side hatch, then he pushes wide the hatch and swims through.

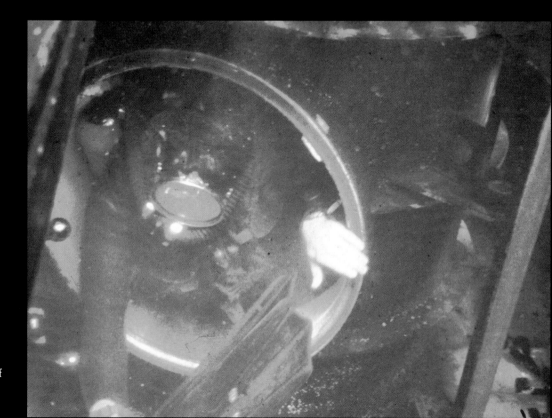

A tight squeeze. A Navy SEAL emerges from the side hatch of an escape trunk at the start of an exercise intended to hone underwater-operations skills.

Retrieving the divers' gear. Working quickly after emerging from the submarine's escape trunk, a Navy SEAL prepares to pull an equipment bag from a storage locker built into the deck of the submarine. The equipment bag, which contains a deflated buoy tethered to a length of sturdy rope known as an ascent-descent line, is kept from being left behind the slowly moving submarine by the lanyard tied to the inside of the locker.

Releasing the buoy. Two SEALs, working as a team, pull the ascent-descent line from the equipment bag and tie it to the submarine, while a third diver, ready to assist if needed, stands by. When the buoy is secure, the divers use a carbon dioxide cartridge to partially inflate it. Upon release, the buoy ascends, trailing the rope behind it. Steadily decreasing sea pressure allows the gas to expand, fully inflating the buoy by the time it reaches the surface.

Inflating the boat. At left, a line from the bow of the inflatable raiding craft has been shackled to the ascent-descent line to keep the boat from drifting. One SEAL steadies the bundle while another prepares to sever twine wrapped around the boat to prevent it from unrolling in its storage locker aboard the submarine. Below, the divers partially inflate the raft, then cut the lanyard that secures the raiding craft to the sub. The inflatable, expanding as it rises, climbs the ascent-descent line to the buoy at the surface.

Marking the path. Their raiding craft launched, three divers wait for other SEALs to exit the submarine through the escape trunk and start their trip to the surface. As each man emerges from the hatch, the diver at bottom hands him the ascent-descent line to serve as a guide to the boat on the surface.

Redress in the South Atlantic

Two Royal Marines surrender to Argentine commandos in the Falklands capital of Port Stanley on April 2, 1982. This picture of British humiliation would unify a nation and launch a task force to retake the islands.

In the early hours of April 2, 1982, a powerful Argentine invasion force, after years of diplomatic dispute, invaded the Falkland Islands, a pair of seamount tops in the South Atlantic 1,000 miles from Buenos Aires and 8,000 miles from London, that had been a British Crown colony since the 1830s. The conquest could not be allowed to stand; her majesty's government had made that abundantly clear. Within a week, a task force had set sail for the tip of South America, charged with recapturing the Falklands, East and West.

Aboard the assault ship *Fearless*, task force officers planned how to achieve their objective. Among the group was Lieutenant Colonel Mike Rose, commander of the British Army's 22d Special Air Service Regiment (22 SAS), who made an unusual suggestion: Why not let the SAS take care of it? A squadron of his men, perhaps 100 in all, would descend on the enemy at night in C-130 Hercules transports disguised with Argentine Air Force markings. Performing a "strip-landing" assault on the Port Stanley airfield, they would race down the rear ramps of the still-taxiing C-130s in machine-gun-equipped Land Rovers. Thence, they would speed into the Falklands' capital, where they would slay or otherwise subdue the members of the Argentine high command in their headquarters billets. Once that was done, the colonel reckoned, the stunned and leaderless Argentines would collapse, and the issue would be resolved.

Colonel Rose, a flint-hard, forty-two-year-old veteran of SAS service the world over, may not have sought approval for the idea from SAS director Brigadier Peter de la Billière, who later would command British forces in the allied Desert Storm campaign against Iraq. But participants in the shipboard strategy sessions later reported that Rose vigorously pressed his views. In the end, the plan proved impractical. And yet, the marvelous audacity of the idea spoke volumes about the SAS and its motto, Who Dares Wins.

Operation Corporate, as the Falklands War was called, would

proceed by more conventional means as a full-scale, combined-services amphibious invasion. Nevertheless, as the campaign unfolded, the SAS and its Royal Marine counterpart, the Special Boat Squadron, would play a critical role and embark on prolonged periods of danger and harrowing hardship that made Rose's idea for an Entebbe-style raid seem tame by comparison.

During the seven violent weeks of the Falklands War, the tough, endlessly resourceful special-operations troops would land by helicopter or in small boats on one of the world's least inviting landscapes. They would endure killing cold and screaming wind, hiding by day in caves or in shallow pits dug in icy peat bogs, emerging at night like scruffy ghosts to scout and harass the enemy; and though no one would admit it, they would even operate on the Argentine mainland. On South Georgia Island, 900 miles east of the main objective and also seized by the Argentines, they and a handful of Royal Marines would launch a little invasion of their own that would effect the surrender of the enemy garrison; remorselessly tracking the enemy on the Falklands, they would call down devastating fire on the Argentine helicopter force, destroy a squadron of attack aircraft before the planes could do any damage, scout the invasion beaches, and then stage a pyrotechnic D-day diversionary demonstration. Finally, at the conclusion, it would be the SAS, with its special psychological warfare skills, that would play a crucial role in negotiating the Argentine surrender. And all this, remarkably, would be the work of units that at no time during the war would number more than 250 men.

For Britain's special-operations forces, the war in the frozen Falklands was the culmination of an idea spawned more than forty years earlier in the searing heat of the North African desert, where a subaltern (later a colonel) named David Stirling was instrumental in selling General Sir Claude Auchinleck, the British commander in the Middle East, on the notion that small teams could parachute far behind enemy lines to sabotage airfields and other installations. The Special Air Service was the Army's response to Stirling's brainstorm. Operating not only in North Africa but in Europe and elsewhere, the SAS eventually earned the malevolent regard of Adolf Hitler. "These men are dangerous," he declared. "They must be hunted down and destroyed at all costs."

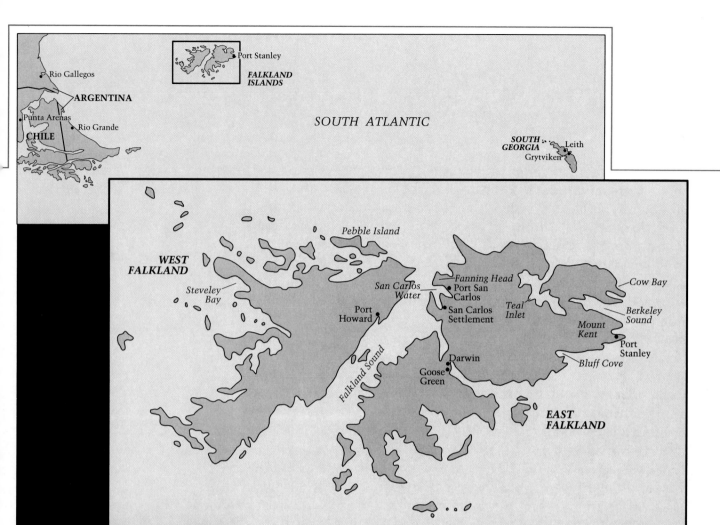

The arena of conflict in the South Atlantic stretched from South Georgia to the Falkland Islands themselves and on to the mainland of Argentina. For Britain's Special Air Service and Special Boat Squadron, the war would begin on the remote and desolate island of South Georgia, 900 miles east of the main islands. Special-operations teams would also land on the South American mainland in an operation still shrouded in official secrecy. But most of the action would take place on East Falkland. From the landings at San Carlos to the retaking of Port Stanley, the men of the SAS and the SBS would play key roles.

During the decades following World War II, the SAS pursued adventurous roles in the jungles of Malaya and Borneo, in the bush of Gambia, and in the mountains of Oman and the murderous back streets of Belfast. In 1977, assisting West German authorities in their rescue of hostages aboard a hijacked Lufthansa airliner that had landed in Somalia, SAS men introduced the stun grenade to the arsenal of counterterrorist weaponry. From time to time, British penal authorities ask the SAS to test various electronic fences, reinforced doors, and other security systems contemplated for use in her majesty's prisons; as often as not, the SAS men send the designers back to the drawing board. And in 1980, the secretive SAS got some undesired publicity when millions of televiewers watched one of its teams, Mike Rose commanding, storm the terrorist-held Iranian embassy in London; it took all of eleven minutes for the SAS to slay or capture the six terrorists and rescue nineteen hostages.

In choosing men who can—and will—carry out such diverse and dangerous missions, the SAS has its pick of the entire British Army. Volunteers are subjected to a four-week course designed not only to strain their physical capabilities but to measure their psychological responses to a series of diabolically designed problems in field operations. Those who succeed in demonstrating their ingenuity,

31

their stamina, their ability to work as part of a small team, and above all, their perseverance in the face of even the most daunting difficulties are then given a further six months of "continuation training" in SAS tactics, parachuting, combat survival, escape and evasion, and interrogation techniques. Only the survivors—as few as 15 percent of all applicants—are at last allowed to wear the winged-dagger badge and the beige beret of the Special Air Service.

In its modern form, the SAS is built to achieve maximum flexibility. Of its three regiments, only one, the 22d, is a full-time, regular outfit; the other two belong to the Territorial Army of reservists. The 22d is composed of four squadrons, each divided into four twelve- to twenty-man troops: a boat troop; a mountain troop; a free-fall troop that specializes in HALO, or high-altitude, low-opening jumps; and a mobility troop of experts in all manner of military vehicles, most particularly those of potential enemies.

The basic unit remains the four-man patrol envisioned by David Stirling. In addition to possessing such SAS-wide skills as parachuting, intelligence gathering and communications, unarmed combat, and competence in the use of a wide variety of weapons, each member of a patrol has his own specialty: concealment, high explosives, auto theft, first aid—any one of a dozen useful talents.

Among the world's special-operations units, the SAS is one of the most secretive. Even so, its reticence pales before that of the Special Boat Squadron of the Royal Marines. While the market town of Hereford is widely known as home to the 22d SAS, few recognize the modest cluster of barracks and boathouses, fronted by a sign that declares the presence of the Amphibious Warfare Training Centre, near the southern seaside resort of Poole, as the headquarters of the SBS. The overall strength (probably fewer than 200) and organization of the SBS are closely held secrets. In their rare contacts with the public, SBS officers and men go by pseudonyms. No public announcements are made when SBS men are awarded medals, and even the squadron's whimsical insignia—a frog with crossed canoe paddles—is worn only at private SBS functions.

Operating under the motto By Guile, Not Strength, the SBS recruits solely from the elite Royal Marines, and even then it accepts only about one of every twenty-five volunteers. Unlike the SAS, which sometimes operates in larger groups, members of the SBS almost always work in four-man teams. As a branch of the Royal Navy, the SBS performs such missions as scouting landing beaches and sabotaging enemy shipping and coastal installations. SBS operatives are trained in such sundry skills as testing beach sand to determine its load-bearing capacity and attaching underwater limpet mines to the hulls of enemy vessels. In one well-practiced scenario, SBS teams make a "wet" parachute drop into the open sea and are taken aboard a waiting submarine, which then transports them close enough to a beach to enable them to swim secretly ashore or land in collapsible, two-man Klepper canoes or inflatable Gemini boats. "We can do anything the SAS does," say SBS men in a boast hotly disputed by the rival force, "and walk on water too."

Unlike members of other British services, the men of both the SBS and the SAS are allowed a wide choice of individual arms. Indeed, said one man, these warriors would be perfectly willing—and able—to use "an ax if that's what's needed." In the Falklands, however, the weapons were far less primitive. Among firearms, the eight-pound, 5.56-mm M16 assault rifle from America was at first universally preferred to the eleven-pound, 7.62-mm British self-loading rifle, but some men switched to the heavier weapon after reports of an Argentine soldier still alive and dangerous after seven hits from the smaller-caliber rifle. In addition, special-operations troopers in the Falklands bristled with a lethal array of knives, pistols, pump-action shotguns, and M79 grenade launchers capable of firing a 40-mm missile to a distance of more than 400 yards.

Inevitably among such outfits, competition is intense. Yet as they ventured forth on their mission to the Falklands, the rivalry was tempered by mutual respect and a sense of shared goals. All were imbued with the spirit embodied in the words—peculiarly appropriate to their remote destination—inscribed on an SAS monument in Hereford: "We are the Pilgrims, Master: / We shall go always a little further: / It may be beyond that last blue mountain barr'd with snow, / Across that angry or that glimmering Sea."

The Argentine invasion was scarcely three days old before the SAS and SBS were on their way to the Falklands. On April 5, four RAF transports embarked sixty-six men of the 22d Regiment's D Squadron and took off for Ascension Island. This minuscule lump of lava about halfway between Great Britain and the Falklands would serve as an assembly point; several days would be gained over the alternative, gathering first in Britain.

Also on board the big planes were 14 SAS radio operators and 50,000 pounds of equipment that the regiment always keeps pre-packed on pallets, ready to go in case of crisis. Next day, accompanied by Colonel Rose and his headquarters staff, G Squadron enplaned for Ascension, bringing the SAS total to about 125; meanwhile, 20 men of the Special Boat Squadron's Two Section, which had recently completed three months of arctic training in Norway, also were flown to Ascension, and another six four-man teams of Six Section were crowded into the nuclear attack submarine *Conqueror*, heading for the South Atlantic at full speed.

On April 10, the first offensive action began; appropriately, it was largely a special-forces show. Departing Ascension, a small fleet composed of the destroyers *Antrim* and *Plymouth* and the tanker *Tidespring* headed south carrying members of the special forces and 120 men of M Company, 42 Commando, Royal Marines. As it plowed through heavy seas, the group was joined by the bright red ice patrol vessel *Endurance*, which had been on duty off the Falklands at the time of the Argentine invasion and had been ordered to remain in the area. Then the flotilla continued to steer south, carefully threading its way through waters infested with enormous icebergs. Its destination was not the Falklands, but South Georgia.

As bleak a piece of real estate as exists on the planet, South Georgia consists largely of crevassed glaciers swept by monstrous winds howling down from the heights. In April 1982, the island's human inhabitants comprised a small contingent of Argentine occupiers, a few Argentine scrap-iron workers imported to dismantle an old whaling station, and thirteen members of a British Antarctic Survey team, who were now playing hide-and-seek with the enemy.

South Georgia might easily have been bypassed, but the island offered a quick and easy victory that would satisfy Britain's thirst for good news from the South Atlantic. Originally, the operation had been code-named Paraquet—which the troops immediately amended to Operation Paraquat, after a well-known weed-killer.

Their grim humor aside, the special-forces operators seemed a rather disreputable lot: Their hair was far longer than regulations permitted; on operations they often went unshaven; and, instead of uniforms, they wore whatever seemed suitable for the conditions. Now they dressed in heavy Norwegian army shirts, turtleneck sweaters, and quilted smocks and trousers. A black watch cap or a balaclava ski mask kept the head warm. Moreover, the SAS and SBS

A Most Remarkable Boat

Waterborne special operations—beach reconnaissance, ship attack, sabotage—usually require a combination of stealth, speed, and the ability to transport essential equipment. For such missions, SEAL and SBS teams among others can call on a variety of small boats, but none is more versatile than Britain's Subskimmer. As shown on the following pages, the Subskimmer is not only a speedy surface craft but also a submersible that can operate partially or completely below the surface.

Such flexibility is the primary advantage of the Subskimmer. A 90-hp outboard engine permits a top speed of twenty-five knots. With a range of seventy nautical miles, the vessel is capable of rapid approaches from considerable distances. As the boat draws closer to a target, a more covert tack may be needed. The Subskimmer obliges by leaving the surface. When partially submerged, the boat uses its snorkel-equipped outboard engine. Maximum speed is two knots to prevent the wake from stripping away the divers' face masks. When fully submerged, the vessel is driven by a pair of battery-powered electric motors. An endurance of nearly three hours allows the last three miles of an approach to be made underwater and undetected with enough battery reserve to withdraw just as discreetly.

Half airborne and slapping against the swell, a Subskimmer manned by a pair of divers dashes across open water.

Classed as a rigid-hull inflatable, this adaptable craft can carry as many as four commandos, yet it can be handled by one.

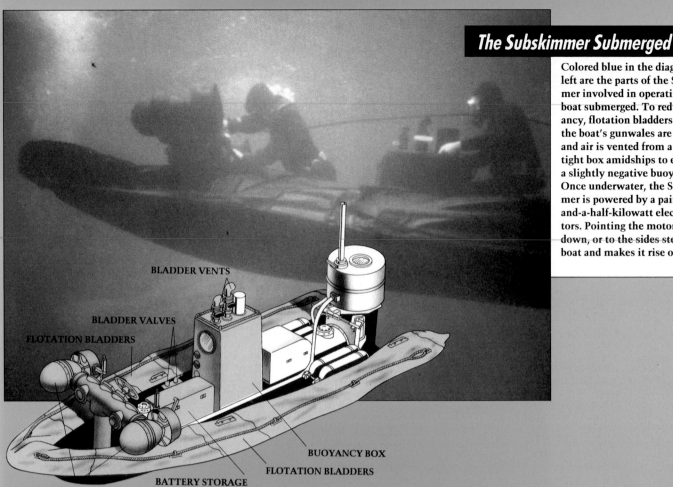

The Subskimmer Submerged

Colored blue in the diagram at left are the parts of the Subskimmer involved in operating the boat submerged. To reduce buoyancy, flotation bladders forming the boat's gunwales are deflated and air is vented from a watertight box amidships to establish a slightly negative buoyancy. Once underwater, the Subskimmer is powered by a pair of one-and-a-half-kilowatt electric motors. Pointing the motors up, down, or to the sides steers the boat and makes it rise or descend.

BLADDER VENTS

BLADDER VALVES

FLOTATION BLADDERS

BUOYANCY BOX

FLOTATION BLADDERS

ELECTRIC MOTORS

BATTERY STORAGE

Snorkeling, Decks Awash

To operate the Subskimmer partially submerged, the driver adjusts buoyancy until the boat floats just beneath the surface. Compressed air, stored in tanks astern, forces water from the buoyancy box to lighten the boat when ascending from below the surface. The driver can choose either the electric motors or the outboard. A snorkel to supply air and a waterproof cowl permit the engine to function even though submerged.

AIR TANKS

SNORKEL

OUTBOARD ENGINE

A Fast Getaway

The Subskimmer can ride on the surface without benefit of its flotation bladders, which take approximately three or four minutes to fill with air. To use this feature, which expedites a retreat, the driver purges all water from the buoyancy box, then accelerates with the outboard. As the boat gathers speed, the force of the water against the hull lifts it onto the surface. The flotation bladders are inflated under way, improving speed and fuel efficiency.

Skipping across the Surface

For optimum performance on the surface, the Subskimmer operates with the buoyancy box empty of water and flotation bladders fully inflated. Of the three bladders—one around the bow and one along each side—the forward chamber is always inflated first to keep from burying the bow in the water.

BOW BLADDER

SIDE BLADDER

officers wore no rank insignia and were always addressed as "boss" instead of the customary "sir." "It was always hard to tell who were officers and who were men," said one observer. "Some of the naval officers began to worry that they were bringing ordinary men into the wardroom, rather than officers. But none of them ever dared challenge the SBS, who had a slight air of menace about them."

As the British ships neared South Georgia, planning sessions in the *Antrim*'s operations room grew intense—and sometimes heated. In overall command of the land forces was Marine Major Guy Sheridan, who persisted in trying to give Major Cedric Delves, commander of both SAS D Squadron and the SBS members appointed to this mission, unwelcome advice on how to achieve the objectives assigned to his troops. Almost intuitively, Delves resisted. "We prefer to be given a task with stated operating parameters," he said later, "and then to be allowed to get on with it."

There was no argument from Delves that Sheridan's Marines and part of the special forces would make the main assault. But first the SAS and SBS would need to reconnoiter landing sites and likely enemy positions: specifically, the SBS was assigned to scout in the vicinity of Grytviken and the British Antarctic Survey station on South Georgia's east coast, while the SAS would check out the whaling station at Leith, thirteen miles farther north.

There, however, agreement ended. The SAS thrives on surprise— and in any case, admits no end to what its men can do. Delves planned to insert his team in the least likely place—atop Fortuna Glacier, a huge mass of ice and snow with five frozen fingers reaching down to the sea. After landing by helicopter, the men would trek across the glacier's 1,800-foot-high dome to a position overlooking Leith. Sheridan, however, recommended against this approach. A skier and mountaineer with experience in the Himalayas, he well knew the difficulties of movement in snow and ice and, as he recorded in his diary, he urged the SAS "on my own experience, to avoid glaciers like the plague." This good advice went unheeded.

At about 1:00 p.m. on April 21, three Wessex helicopters lifted off the *Antrim* carrying D Squadron's sixteen-man mountain troop, commanded by Captain John Hamilton. The weather was foul, with wind gusts registering sixty miles per hour. "There was simply no horizon," recalled a pilot who had groped for a landing spot atop the glacier. "Ice, snow, and cloud all blended into one."

Somehow the choppers got down, unloaded the SAS teams and

their gear, and took off again. Now alone on the glacier, the SAS men roped themselves together in groups of three and four, then struggled into the harnesses of sleds brought along to transport supplies. According to plan, the group was expected to march two miles and get off the glacier by nightfall. But as soon as the troopers set out, they knew that they were in trouble. Every thirty yards or so, a man would plunge up to his waist in a snow-concealed crevasse and have to be hauled out by his mates. Yet on they pressed, each man leaning against the gale, each man gasping for breath. After five agonizing hours, the party had progressed scarcely 800 yards—and there was no choice but to bed down on the glacier.

It was a nightmare. Since tents would not stand against a wind now screeching at up to 100 miles per hour, the troopers used ice axes to hack out shallow two-man trenches and wrapped themselves in the tents' nylon as protection against the storm's blasts. Even so, snow threatened to bury them as they attempted to sleep, and every forty-five minutes or so they had to get up and dig out. When morning finally arrived, conditions were no better, movement was impossible, and Captain Hamilton reluctantly signaled that the SAS mountain troop would have to be airlifted off the glacier—that is, if rescue was even possible.

At 10:50 a.m., the three choppers again lifted off from the *Antrim* and spent half an hour fighting in vain against gusting headwinds to reach the altitude of the stranded SAS men. The pilots tried again at 1:30 p.m., and this time they made it through the clouds and blowing snow. Taking six of the suffering troops aboard, a twin-engined Wessex 5 staggered aloft and headed for the glacier's rim. Almost immediately, the craft was hit by a vicious snow squall, and its pilot suffered the phenomenon known as whiteout, dreaded by all fliers in frigid regions. "It's like trying to see through milk," one pilot has explained. "You become disoriented." After traveling less than a mile, the helicopter fell out of the sky from forty feet and hit hard, its left undercarriage ripped away by the impact.

Amazingly, no one was killed or even seriously hurt, and the two remaining choppers immediately flew to the crash site to pick up the downed men. A single-engined Wessex 3 piloted by Lieutenant Commander Ian Stanley, with one SAS man already on board, packed a crewman and two troopers into its cramped cabin, while a twin-engined Wessex 5 added a crewman and the remaining four soldiers to the nine semifrozen individuals in the cabin. Since Stanley's bird was the better instrumented, he led the attempt to break the glacier's grip. As the two helicopters labored aloft, Stanley's copilot peered back through the port cockpit window at the trailing helicopter. "Fine, okay, okay, following us at fifty yards, steady, steady, steady, all okay," he intoned. And then: "Oh, God! He's gone in!" The pilot of the second chopper had encountered another whiteout—and had crashed from seventy feet of altitude. Even now, there were no casualties, but two precious helicopters were clearly out of commission, and when Stanley arrived safely on the *Antrim* with three SAS passengers, there were still thirteen men, plus three aircrew, left on the glacier. If forced to spend another night on the icy massif, some of them would surely be dead next morning.

By 4:00 p.m., the ferocity of the storm seemed to diminish, and Stanley took off again. Searching for a hole in the clouds, he "stooged around for a few minutes and then, in a sudden break, we were looking straight down at a crashed helicopter. I dived down through the gap and landed alongside." But now the weather was again closing in and Stanley knew that there would not be another chance before nightfall. The only hope was to take everybody in a single lift; with Stanley and his copilot that meant eighteen men in

On the afternoon of April 22, four cold and dejected members of an SAS mountain troop cautiously make their way across the ice of South Georgia's Fortuna Glacier to aid the survivors of a helicopter crash. Footing on the glacier was treacherous; the last man in line is struggling to his feet after punching through the ice.

a helicopter whose capacity was supposed to be less than half that number. "When we took off," one of the SAS troopers later recalled, "there were arms and legs sticking out of the door and windows."

They just made it. Stanley brought the barely flyable craft, sinking almost as fast as the glacier sloped away beneath it, down on the *Antrim* in what one observer called "a bloody marvelous controlled crash landing." That night

the troopers presented Stanley with a bottle of whiskey. It was their way of saying that he was, in spirit if not in fact, one of their own.

Meanwhile, the SBS was having its own dramatic difficulties, and for a time it seemed as if the entire operation to retake South Georgia was jinxed. The idea was to insert three four-man SBS patrols by helicopter from HMS *Endurance* some distance from Grytviken; the men would trek to a rendezvous, where the chopper would bring in a pair of Gemini boats in which they could approach their objective across a broad bay. But the atrocious weather threw the timetable out of kilter, and when the helicopter at last arrived with the Geminis swaying beneath in cargo slings, it came in so low that one of the boats slammed into a rock and was too badly holed to use.

With one Gemini ruined and the seas too rough for the remaining craft to carry more than four, two of the patrols had to stay behind while the third set off in the sound boat—and motored into a horrific vista. A nearby glacier, two miles wide and 100 feet high, was shedding thousands of tons of ice, until the water, said an SBS Marine, "was packed really tight—bits of ice of all shapes and sizes—growlers, icebergs, and brash." There appeared to be only one narrow channel, and the men went for it. But not for long. "We managed to cover about 800 yards when it became obvious that we

After a second helicopter crash atop the glacier, an aircrewman and two SAS troopers break out a life raft for use as a temporary shelter while they await rescue by the last remaining helicopter. In high winds and driving snow, only the massed weight of the men curled up inside them prevented the inflated boats from being blown away.

were in trouble," recalled one of the men. With five miles still to go, the wind was rising and the channel was closing. The Gemini's outboard was straining hard. If the engine died, explained another, "then we would be swept back onto the ice and crushed to bits. There was no way you could climb onto that stuff, or try to walk across it." The crossing was reluctantly abandoned, and the next night the SBS group was evacuated by helicopter.

Two attempts. Two failures. Yet the special forces are imbued with unswerving persistence in the face of crushing discouragement. By the time his mountain troop returned from the Fortuna Glacier, Major Delves was already making plans to put the squadron's boat troop onto South Georgia. And that he eventually did, sending out fifteen men in five Geminis from the *Antrim* to a position from which they could climb to high ground above Leith. Though assiduously seaproofed, the outboard engines clamped to the Gemini transoms were notoriously fickle. True to their reputation, two of them conked out in the brutal weather and would not be restarted. One of the boats would drift until the next day before being found by the guardian angel helicopter pilot Lieutenant Commander Stanley. The other was driven ashore, where its occupants would camp five days in a cave before being picked up. By that time, the South Georgia campaign would be over.

The three other Geminis, however, made it to their objective, and by the morning of April 24, a patrol of SAS men was at last on a hill overlooking the settlement of Leith and the enemy garrison. There, they watched with great interest as an officer inspected the Argentine trenches, thereby pinpointing defensive positions. But when the SAS radioed its news to the *Antrim*, the men were informed that fast-moving events at Grytviken had made it unlikely that Leith would be the point of invasion.

A Brief Scare from the Depths

While the special-operations troopers were struggling to reconnoiter the bleak terrain of South Georgia, Royal Navy commanders were severely jolted by the report of an Argentine submarine in the vicinity. Leaving only the *Endurance* to support the troops that had been sent ashore, the tiny fleet ran for cover amid icebergs 200 miles to the north. The *Antrim* and the *Plymouth* soon returned, but the highly vulnerable *Tidespring* remained behind—with nearly all the Marines of M Company.

Then, on April 25, the *Antrim's* surviving Wessex—flying an antisubmarine patrol and once again piloted by Ian Stanley—spotted the enemy submersible making its way out of the harbor at Grytviken. Stanley was able to identify the vessel as the *Santa Fe,* a World War II diesel-powered submarine that had been purchased by Argentina from the United States. The boat was on the surface, a sub hunter's dream come true. Swooping into the attack, Stanley dropped a pair of 250-pound depth charges close aboard. Helicopters from the other British ships hammered the submarine with rockets, and the hapless *Santa Fe,* spewing smoke and trailing a wake of oil, was run aground.

Aboard the *Antrim,* the Royal Marines' Major Sheridan knew an opportunity when he saw it. Calculating that the sub's demise would demoralize the enemy garrison, Sheridan urged an immediate invasion with whatever force could be thrown together. Even though little was known of the enemy's disposition, the SAS's Cedric Delves enthusiastically agreed, and Sheridan quickly organized a group of seventy-five men from his own headquarters, from Royal Marines who were serving as part of the ships' companies, and from the Special Air Service and Special Boat Squadron.

Now, after all the adversity, all the frustrations, all the pain inflicted by the hostile elements, the unswerving perseverance that is a hallmark of the special-operations troops finally paid off with bewildering rapidity. At 2:45 p.m. on April 25, helicopters began landing the patchwork British assault force approximately three miles from Grytviken. As the British soldiers worked their way over the shoulder of a small mountain, the *Antrim* and the *Plymouth* laid down a creeping barrage of naval gunfire that drew closer and closer to the Argentine garrison.

By the time the attacking force came within sight of Grytviken, a number of white flags were already waving from the settlement. With three other men, Delves moved cautiously down the steep slope. "We passed through the old whaling station," he recalled, "and went along the narrow track. We passed a machine-gun post—the crew just standing there with their arms in the air and looking nervous—and I said, 'Good afternoon. How do you do?'"

The next day, Leith surrendered as well, and the British had in their hands a total of 185 Argentine prisoners. When the news reached London, Prime Minister Margaret Thatcher appeared on the front steps of No. 10 Downing Street. "Rejoice!" she called to waiting newsmen. "Just rejoice!"

But there was no resting on laurels. Hardly had they secured South Georgia than the SAS and SBS detachments transferred to destroyers that raced to join the main invasion force for Operation Corporate, now plowing south through the Atlantic from the staging base at Ascension Island.

The fleet had sailed from Ascension on April 18. By April 30, it had reached a point about 200 miles off the Falklands, and even at that late date the question of where the invading troops should go ashore was still unanswered. Though the British had intimate knowledge of the islands with their 14,913 miles of coastline, the task force planners knew little as yet of enemy emplacements and strengths. At one time or another, commanders aboard the assault ship *Fearless* discussed the virtues and drawbacks of as many as thirty different landing sites. Gradually, the list of possibilities was whittled down to a dozen, then to five. With the Argentines still in control of the clouded Falklands skies, a thorough aerial reconnaissance was clearly out of the question, and the British had to rely entirely on the special-operations teams to reconnoiter the beaches and pinpoint the enemy forces.

Insertions began on the night of May 1, when Sea King HC-4 helicopters from the aircraft carrier *Hermes* skimmed almost at wave-top height on a perilous three-hour flight to deposit the first of eight four-man SAS patrols and six four-man SBS teams at widely dispersed points on both islands. "We started out with a blank map of the Falklands," recalled the Royal Marines' Brigadier Julian Thompson, commanding the main landing force, "and fired special forces like a shotgun across the islands to see what they found."

With sounds of engines and whipping rotors masked by a howling wind, the Sea King pilots came whirling in from the sea and searched out their assigned destinations with the aid of night-vision goggles acquired from the United States. The men who jumped out could hardly have liked what little they saw, but their rough and boggy training areas at home had prepared them for it. Although the Falklands are studded by mountains whose slopes offer caves and clusters of boulders to hide among, the land is mostly open, treeless

44

A Wasp helicopter from HMS *Endurance* hovers near the disabled Argentine submarine *Santa Fe,* down at the stern in Grytviken harbor after the SAS-led liberation of South Georgia. The victory was a boost for the British forces in the Falklands and a foretaste of the stiffer challenge yet to come.

moor with no concealment whatever. And no one could be sure about the caliber of the Argentines; many were said to be raw conscripts, but there also were reports of very tough, very well equipped special-operations units, perhaps the equal of the SBS and the SAS. "No one knew how good they were," explained one trooper, "or whether there wouldn't be a reception party to scarf you up."

As always, the British sought to disguise their intentions by landing the reconnaissance teams as much as a forty-eight-hour march from their objectives. Given the Argentines' control of the air, they could move only at night across the treacherous, marshy terrain. And so they set out, doggedly feeling their way through the darkness, unable to light even a match for illumination, constantly lashed by high winds and frequently pummeled by driving rain and sleet, toward the positions from which they would conduct their clandestine investigations. At the first glimmer of daylight, they would go to ground, digging shallow trenches that they would cover with chicken wire and layers of peat turf.

When they at last crept into their observation posts, the patrols found that their difficulties had only begun. Among the major problems was a lack of up-to-date communications equipment: Budgetary restrictions had prevented Britain's special-operations units from obtaining modern burst-transmission radios that could compress long messages into single squawks lasting less than ten seconds. Instead, the scouts were forced to rely on traditional Morse, a slow way of signaling and one that made them vulnerable to enemy radio direction finders.

On at least one occasion, members of an SAS team were so fearful of being discovered that they did not make even the brief daily report required to inform seaborne commanders that the group was still alive and working. Finally, after two days and just as officers on the *Fearless* were beginning to worry in earnest, a message came through advising that the team had been holed up in the middle of an Argentine troop concentration.

As for the long, detailed reports essential for invasion planning, they were too perilous even to try. Instead, couriers, and sometimes the entire team, had to make two- or three-night marches away from their observation posts so helicopters could fly them out to the *Fearless*, where they delivered their assessments in person.

Just before one SBS team was about to be extracted, a man became separated in the darkness from the rest of the group. Forced to leave without him—under no circumstances could a helicopter linger for long in the hostile vicinity—the three other members were lifted to the fleet, where they were lengthily debriefed, and resupplied with rations and ammunition. When they returned to East Falkland, they found the missing man at one of several predesignated rendezvous points, calmly awaiting their arrival after surviving a week in the frozen, enemy-infested wilderness.

For the SAS teams, the main jobs were to ascertain the areas where the Argentines had concentrated their strength, to map trench systems and artillery positions, to locate airstrips being used by Argentine warplanes, and to assess the condition of the enemy's soldiers on matters ranging from weaponry to health and morale.

The SAS teams painted an encouraging picture of the Argentine soldiers. They were, to be sure, well armed with fully automatic rifles; they also were amply supplied with mobile, Italian-made 105-mm howitzers, and their night-fighting optical equipment was superior to anything the British had. Yet except for a few SAS-style units, the Argentine troops were, as expected, mainly conscripts best described by one British commander as "sloppy, disinterested, and dozy," and the watching SAS groups were pleased to note that they were neglectful of even such soldierly hygiene as washing and changing their clothes.

Scouting the Beach

As valuable as such observations were, the more urgent need was to select a place for the invasion force to go ashore. That assignment fell largely to the SBS, whose teams swiftly and silently set about determining which of the five potential landing sites had the best of the following attributes: a sheltered stretch of coast, beaches that were shelved steeply enough so landing craft could come close ashore and firm enough to take heavy equipment, good exit routes from the beachheads for tracked and wheeled vehicles, and, of course, an absence of Argentine defenders.

When the SBS reports began coming in, the possibilities were eliminated one by one. Steveley Bay on West Falkland seemed ideal except for one thing: Starting there would require crossing Falkland Sound to East Falkland, where the main enemy body was entrenched. Port Stanley itself was tempting as a place to end the war quickly, but the Argentine defenders in the area would outnumber the landing force by nearly three to one. Berkeley Sound, ten miles above Port Stanley, and Cow Bay, even farther north, fell by the wayside after intelligence indicated that they were heavily mined.

That left San Carlos Water, fifty miles across country from Port Stanley on the west coast of East Falkland. And during the first ten days of May, planners aboard the *Fearless* focused on reports from an SBS team operating in the San Carlos environs.

The four-man group, led by a thirty-six-year-old sergeant, was inserted by helicopter about ten miles from the spot where it intended to set up its observation post. Three nights later, the team members concealed themselves in a cave amid a jumble of rocks on a ridge overlooking the inlet of San Carlos Water and the tiny communities of Port San Carlos and San Carlos Settlement.

By day, the members of the team remained on the ridge, taking turns sleeping and venturing from their cave to lie in shallow scrapes dug into the earth and expertly camouflaged. From these hides, they could peer through binoculars and a sixty-power telescope at the scene below. Against all expectations, there was little enemy activity—no garrison, no traffic on the grass airstrip near San Carlos, only an occasional patrol that gave a desultory look around before departing. Still, on at least one occasion the sergeant had a harrowing experience. Lying prone in a camouflaged trench, he listened worriedly to the unmistakable sound of an approaching helicopter. Closer and closer it came, until it was directly above him. And there, for several minutes, it hovered, so low that the downdraft from its rotary blades began blowing away the bits of turf that the sergeant was using as cover. Then, at last, the chopper flew away: Evidently trying to get his bearings, the pilot had presumably looked in every direction but straight down.

At night, the team descended from its hillside observation post to explore beaches, settlements, and other points of military interest. Unfortunately, the shore was so rocky that landing craft could not beach to let the troops off. The attackers would probably have to splash the last few yards from the landing craft. Marines, of course, were used to wet feet, but in the dank Falklands winter, feet would not dry until after the campaign. Many men would suffer from the fungus affliction known as trench foot. Otherwise, the SBS reported, the anchorage was unmined and satisfactorily free of kelp, the entangling seaweed that blights Falklands waters; a surrounding line of hills would offer some protection from storms and a strong defensive perimeter. All in all, Brigadier Thompson decided after digesting the SBS information, San Carlos "provided everything I wanted." Upon his recommendation, the British War Cabinet in London on May 10 authorized the landings at San Carlos.

Almost immediately, a new and unexpected development took place—one, as it turned out, that would give the SAS some of the most satisfying moments of its stay in the Falklands. From the time of the Special Air Service's founding, its franchise had included explosive sabotage and violent action against enemy outposts. Such opportunities had been long acoming in the Falklands, and now one appeared almost by happenstance.

A Harrier pilot from the *Hermes* reported that radar had locked onto his aircraft while flying over Pebble Island, a long, narrow arm of rock just off the northeast coast of West Falkland. Cleaning out a lonely radar station was no more than simple housekeeping for the SAS, and on the evening of May 11, eight men were landed by chopper on the West Falkland mainland, just south of Pebble Island. Their plan: to paddle Klepper canoes across an 800-yard stretch of water, call in heliborne reinforcements, destroy the enemy installation, then withdraw and get on with further business.

But nothing in the Falklands was ever easy. Squalls kicked up choppy waves that thwarted the crossing. Not until the night of May 13, when the weather eased, were the troopers able to make the short trip to Pebble Island. The group split into two four-man squads, and one of them headed toward the island's only settlement, whose twenty-five inhabitants were outnumbered a thousand to one by the sheep that they tended. Nearing the village, the men crossed a ridgeline—and gazed in amazement at an unsuspected airstrip with eleven Argentine planes parked nearby. Protecting the airfield was a garrison of about 100 men.

A good half of the aircraft were twin-turboprop Pucarás, effective ground-attack planes. Developed by Argentina as a counterinsurgency weapon, the Pucará mounted two 20-mm cannons and could deliver 3,300 pounds of rockets, bombs, and napalm. In addition, there were four Turbo-Mentor turboprop light attack planes and a Skyvan transport. By themselves the warplanes probably could not defeat or even seriously impede the British troops going ashore at

The remains of an Argentine Pucará ground-attack plane lie on the airstrip at Pebble Island, one of six such victims of a raid by D Squadron, SAS, during the night of May 14. Though the light, slow-flying turboprops would have been no match for Royal Navy Sea Harriers, the Pucarás were destroyed because of the threat they posed to British helicopters.

San Carlos; the landings would be protected by an umbrella of antiaircraft artillery and missile fire, as well as Sea Harrier jet fighters on combat air patrol. But the Pucará's guns could be murderous against British helicopters operating outside the air-defense umbrella, so when word of the Argentine aircraft was flashed to the fleet, British commanders decided to destroy them forthwith.

The destroyer *Glamorgan* was detached from the main battle force and sent speeding toward Pebble Island, while forty-eight members of the SAS's D Squadron, led by Cedric Delves, took off from the *Hermes* in three Westland Commando Mark 22 helicopters. Accompanying the SAS contingent was an observer from 148 Forward Observation Battery, 29 Commando Regiment, Royal Artillery—a unit that would work closely with special-operations forces throughout the war. The observer's job would be to correct the aim of the destroyer's guns.

As evening fell on May 14, a Friday—a favored time for special

operations, on the theory that enemies tend to relax on weekends—the raiders landed at a spot marked by the teams that had preceded them. Then they marched hurriedly the five miles to the airfield and poised themselves on its perimeter. At a signal from the observer, the *Glamorgan,* by now lying close offshore, sent up star shells to illuminate the enemy planes. Then, as the destroyer laid down fire to pin the Argentine garrison in its quarters about a half-mile away, the SAS troopers sprinted onto the airstrip and ran down the line of planes hurling incendiary grenades; blasting away with assault rifles, 40-mm grenade launchers, and 66-mm antiarmor rockets; and tossing plastic explosives between the wheels.

It was a classic "bash and dash action," as one officer put it, "the chance to go in and cause a bit of trouble, then get out fast." The mission was scheduled to last fifteen minutes. But it was the sort of thing the SAS had not had a chance to enjoy since World War II, and half an hour passed with the men still racing up and down the line of planes, making sure of everything. "Three times they were told to stop having a good time and get the hell out of it," said Colonel Mike Rose later, "and three times there was some strangely suspicious reason why they never got the order."

When the raiders at last began to withdraw, some Argentines mounted a meager counterattack led by a wildly gesticulating officer. The SAS cut him down, and with their leader dead, the enemy soldiers fled. Days later, an officer of the Royal Marines would draw a lesson from that incident. "When you're shooting people," he told his own troops, "pick the man who is waving his arms about."

At a cost of two minor casualties—an Argentine mine, set off by remote control, injured one man; the other took a bullet in the leg—D Squadron had destroyed all eleven aircraft on Pebble Island—along with an ammunition dump, a fueling facility, and the radar station that had brought them there in the first place.

The triumph at the airfield showed that surprise, backed by ample firepower, is often a decisive factor in battle. Unfortunately, the unexpected can cut the other way as well, and the enemy need not play a role. Five days after reducing the Argentine aircraft on Pebble Island to smoldering carcasses, a Sea King helicopter clattered off the *Hermes* to transfer a contingent of twenty-five SAS troopers to the assault ship *Intrepid* steaming less than a mile away. While circling the *Intrepid* in preparation for landing, the pilots suddenly heard two loud reports from one of the engines. The chopper immediately lost power and plunged into the sea. Only six men survived, including one trooper, who related that his foot had been inextricably caught in some webbing. Then he felt a hand grasp his ankle, followed by a sawing movement and two firm taps on his foot to tell him that he was free. No one will ever know who performed that selfless act, for he was among the nineteen SAS men who, along with an aircrewman and a forward air controller from the RAF, died that afternoon. Their average age was thirty-four, all of them career noncommissioned officers of long experience, the cream of the SAS. Wrote Rose stoically in his report: "The Regiment has taken it well and are getting on with the fighting at present."

Indeed that was so, for another SAS triumph was in the making. One of the several teams inserted early in May was an SAS patrol under Captain Aldwin Wight. While others had been scouting amphibious-landing sites, Wight and his men had taken a position on East Falkland, in the hills overlooking Port Stanley. There, the Argentine commander, Major General Mario Menendez, had concentrated the great majority of his 12,000-man force. Day after day,

Two helicopters approach the carrier *Hermes* on May 19 to pick up SAS troopers destined for the assault ship *Intrepid,* as the British prepare for the main landings on East Falkland. During one such "crossdecking" operation just hours later, a Sea King helicopter crashed into the sea, killing nineteen. It was the regiment's single greatest loss since World War II.

the SAS men lay motionless in carefully camouflaged hiding places amid clumps of tussock grass. They soon noticed that each afternoon toward dusk the enemy's Chinook, Puma, Huey, and Bell helicopters took to the air from Port Stanley and beat away toward the west, returning to Port Stanley early the next morning.

Calculating that the Argentines were removing their rotary-wing aircraft from the danger of nighttime British naval bombardment, the SAS team determined to find the nocturnal hideaway. Abandoning the scant comfort of the gravelike trenches in which they slept, the men probed westward. At length, they came upon a secluded saddle of land near Mount Kent, about ten miles from Port Stanley. There were the helicopters.

There was no time for a trek to the coast and a personal report on board the *Fearless*. Withdrawing some distance to reduce the chance of discovery, Wight put himself and his men at huge risk by radioing a call for an air strike. The Argentines may or may not have intercepted the message, but by the time that two RAF GR3 Harrier fighter-bombers sped from the carrier *Hermes* to the grid reference supplied by Wight, the helicopters had been flown away. Disappointed but not defeated, the SAS team started the hunt again,

rediscovering the helicopters—with the same result: The choppers were gone by the time the Harriers arrived.

Destroying these helicopters was becoming a matter of some urgency. The main body of the British force was to begin landing at San Carlos, and these aircraft, heavy lifters all, would be of great help to the Argentines in transporting troops to block the invasion's advance. Wight's patrol continued the search and found the helicopters again on the morning of May 21, just as the landings began. This time, when he summoned the Harriers, they arrived soon enough to catch the choppers on the ground and destroyed a Chinook and two Pumas. The blow considerably reduced the Argentines' ability to reinforce beleaguered positions by air as the British drove inland, and it made General Menendez even more careful about putting his remaining helicopters at risk.

Returning to the hills above Port Stanley, the SAS team resumed its vigil. In all, the men would remain in the field for twenty-six days amid what Wight's citation for the Military Cross later described as "appalling" conditions, with weather that "varied from freezing rain to gale force winds." When finally extracted, the men were weak from their meager diet of dehydrated rations, and because of trench foot induced by the constant damp within their miserable little scrapes, they were scarcely able to walk.

Meanwhile, the SAS was engaged in an operation so secret that years later the very fact of it—to say nothing of any details—remained shrouded in mystery. Though the Pucarás and Turbo-Mentor attack planes were gone, British planners had never regarded local Argentine air assets as the major threat to a successful landing. The tacticians' attention had long been riveted on Argentine aircraft operating from mainland bases within range of the Falklands. It was understood, quite correctly as it turned out, that the Argentine Air Force and Naval Air Arm were both well trained and well equipped, with U.S.-supplied A-4 Skyhawk attack planes and supersonic French-built Mirage IIIE fighter-bombers, along with a handful of very dangerous French Super Etendards capable of launching the sea-skimming, radar-guided Exocet antiship missile, which could be fired from more than twenty-five miles away.

It was politically impossible for the British to launch preemptive attacks against the mainland bases, even if they had the means to strike effectively. The handful of RAF and Navy Harriers—never more than forty-five of them—flying from the small carriers *Hermes* and *Invincible* had little range and no aerial refueling capability for lack of tankers. Their best use would be for combat air patrol over the fleet and the troops ashore. Too few to maintain continuous airborne pickets, the Harriers required timely notice of incoming Argentine air strikes. Taking off from the big Argentine base at Rio Grande, 300 miles from the Falklands, a flight of A-4s, Mirages, or Etendards could be upon the fleet in less than thirty minutes. The Harriers and the shipboard missile batteries needed all of that warning time and more, a requirement far beyond the capabilities of the fleet's radar.

Thus it was that on the night of May 17, with D-day only seventy-two hours away, the *Invincible*, escorted by the destroyer *Broadsword* and with SAS men aboard, broke away from the British task force north of the Falklands and made a high-speed run to the southwest. At 3:15 a.m., a Sea King helicopter was launched from the *Invincible*, then the ships reversed course and rejoined the fleet.

Two days later, the BBC in London blandly announced that a Royal Navy Sea King had "crash-landed" on a beach in Chile, just beyond the Argentine border near the seaport of Punta Arenas. "We were on sea patrol when we experienced engine failure due to adverse weather," said the Sea King's pilot. "It was not possible to return to our ship in these conditions. We therefore took refuge in the nearest neutral country."

Immediately thereafter, British commanders began receiving detailed information on the times, types, and weapons load of Argentine aircraft taking off from Rio Grande. Concurrently, the fleet started getting similar information on the activity at two other Argentine bases farther north along the coast: Rio Gallegos and Comodoro Rivadavia. It is widely believed that the Sea King landed an SAS team near Rio Grande and that the SBS was inserted by submarine at the two northern bases.

On the evening of Thursday, May 20, 1982, as the British battle force waited at sea to begin the transit south to San Carlos Water, men of the Royal Marines and the Parachute Regiment blackened their faces and inspected their gear in preparation for assaulting the beaches at dawn. Yet even then, special-operations forces had vio-

lent chores to perform in opening the way for the invasion.

Earlier that night, a Wessex 5 helicopter had flown a reconnaissance mission over Fanning Head, a barren promontory guarding the entrance to San Carlos Water. Using a thermal imager, a device that measures the smallest differences in heat from objects in the field of view and converts them into images, the pilot had detected the presence of what could only be Argentine troops who had occupied Fanning Head, previously reported by the SBS to be vacant. Clearly, gunfire from this position would gravely endanger the task force as it entered San Carlos Water, so the SBS was detailed to neutralize the threat.

At about 11:00 p.m., thirty-two troopers, armed with a dozen machine guns, were landed by helicopter at a point approximately six miles from the target. They were accompanied by a captain of the Royal Marines named Rod Bell, who spoke fluent Spanish. The officer had brought with him a battery-powered bullhorn in the hope of persuading the Argentines to surrender without bloodshed. But when his proposal went unanswered and a hand-held thermal imager the SBS had brought along showed the eerie figures of men approaching through the night, the British opened fire. After a few minutes, however, Bell persuaded the SBS commander to cease. "We were massacring them," he recalled, "and I wanted to talk again." With two volunteers, he moved toward the enemy outpost—while the SBS sergeant major stomped around angrily muttering, "Gentlemen, this is NOT the way to do business."

As it turned out, the sergeant major was right. The Argentines opened fire, Bell and his companions dived for cover, and the SBS responded with lethal effect. "It was getting daylight now," Bell said later, "and the Argentinians were running up to the highest ground. It was a duck shoot. You could see them falling."

In the event, six enemy soldiers surrendered and three wounded men were taken prisoner. Later, after the invasion force had occupied the area, the Royal Marines found a dozen or so Argentine bodies sprawled on the ground.

While the SBS was killing the enemy on Fanning Head, the SAS drew an assignment to do just the opposite at Darwin and Goose Green, twenty miles to the south of the San Carlos beaches. Earlier reconnaissance of these settlements had identified an Argentine garrison of as many as 500 men. To keep that force in place during the San Carlos landings, 40 SAS men were inserted by helicopter four miles above Darwin with orders that were terse and to the point: "Noise. Firepower. No close engagement."

Following instructions to the letter, the SAS troopers put on a bang-up show, constantly changing firing positions as they let loose with rifles, machine guns, mortars, and Milan rockets in a blazing pyrotechnic display. The Argentine commander, far from realizing that he outnumbered the noisemakers by as many as twelve to one, radioed his superiors that he was under attack by a full 600-man battalion. Whether they believed him is moot. No reinforcements arrived, and the Argentines did not stir from their positions when the first waves of British paratroopers and Marines waded ashore.

SAS and SBS patrols scouted ahead of the regular troops as they began their advance on Port Stanley. There were hazards to being in the vanguard, and they could come from friendlies and hostiles alike. On the stormy night of June 2, a four-man patrol from the SAS's G Squadron was manning a forward observation post when they spotted black-clad figures approaching their position from an area known to be in Argentine hands. When the SAS challenged "Halt!" three of the four men stopped in their tracks, but the fourth

made a dive for cover. A reflexive burst of fire cut him down before he reached the ground.

Only after the incident, when the intruders advanced to be recognized, did the SAS troopers realize that the threatening figures were an SBS patrol unaware that in the rain-swept darkness they had wandered two miles out of their assigned area. The dead soldier was Sergeant I. N. "Kiwi" Hunt, one of the squadron's most experienced and valued men. He was the only SBS fatality of the war.

Eight days later, the SAS, too, lost one of its best. On June 10, D Squadron's redoubtable Captain John Hamilton, more than recovered from his near-disastrous visit to the glacier on South Georgia, was with a four-man patrol above Port Howard on West Falkland. The unit had been sent there to warn of any Argentine effort to attack the British rear. Just after dawn, Hamilton and his radio operator moved out of concealment to get a closer look at some enemy positions. Concentrating on their observations, they did not see an enemy patrol moving in behind them until it was too late. Hamilton and his companion tried to fight their way out with standard SAS "pepper-pot" tactics, a leapfrog style of withdrawal

Two members of the Special Air Service, heads down and M16s at the ready, alight from a Scout helicopter at Bluff Cove, just fifteen miles west of Port Stanley. The mobility that helicopters afforded the SAS and SBS throughout the war was a major factor in the defeat of the largely static Argentine defense.

wherein one man dashes a short distance toward safety while the other lays down covering fire. But the bare hillside provided no shelter, and Hamilton was hit as the radio operator was making his run. "You carry on. I'll cover your back," shouted Hamilton, who blazed away until he was killed. The captain was awarded a posthumous Military Cross for his valor. He lies buried where he fell.

The climax of the war found the SAS employing psychological-warfare tactics often used against terrorists holding hostages. Ever since June 6, Mike Rose had arranged daily broadcasts to Port Stanley over a radio frequency used by the hospital to transmit medical advice to outlying settlements. The channel was monitored by the Argentines, who had kept it open during the occupation. Now the Spanish-speaking Captain Rod Bell had a message for any who might be listening. With 9,500 British troops on the island drawing the noose ever tighter, the Argentine forces were doomed; it would be honorable and humane to surrender without further bloodshed.

For a week the broadcasts continued, but they brought no re-

sponse as the main British force advanced on Port Stanley. On June 13, the SAS suggested mounting a diversion in support of a paratroop attack on Wireless Ridge a few miles west of Port Stanley and the last significant Argentine defenses between Britain and victory.

That night, using four rigid raiders—flat-bottomed, blunt-bowed boats powered by 140-hp outboard engines—a thirty-two-man raiding party composed of SAS men and Royal Marines would dash across Stanley harbor from the southern shore, then land on the north side and generally raise Cain before departing. The operation would emphatically remind the Argentines that they could expect attack at any time from any quarter and perhaps encourage an early surrender. The ever-ready Major Delves, who would command the raiders, even thought that if the enemy collapsed that night or next morning, he and his men might claim the honor of being the first British soldiers to enter the capital—only fitting considering their long tenure in the Falklands.

The men crouched low on the boat thwarts, and helmsmen braced themselves as the rigid raiders sortied into the harbor, pounding through the waves and spray. Hardly had the crossing begun when things went wrong. Crewmen on the *Bahia Paraiso*, an Argentine icebreaker pressed into service as a hospital ship, picked up the boats with the vessel's searchlight. An antiaircraft battery opened up with its 20-mm guns and a coastal defense position joined in with heavy machine-gun and small-arms fire. The helmsmen frantically twisted and turned under the tracer streams and the troopers—off balance, often facing away from the threat because of the boats' gyrations, and apprehensive about accidentally shooting their own—returned fire as best they could. Two of the boats were quickly hit and three men wounded. One rigid raider threw a propeller and had to be taken under tow.

There was nothing for Delves but to abort the mission. He ordered the helmsmen to reverse course and head for home under cover of friendly artillery called down by an alert officer ashore who witnessed the calamity. Holed and splintered, the boats were run up on the beach and the troopers made for the hills, where they were picked up by helicopters a few days later.

Some analysts, expressing skepticism about the need for a diversion, strongly suspect that the aggressive SAS troopers wanted merely to take one final whack at the foe. Yet, while the effort was something of a bust and did nothing to distract enemy attention

Orange smoke and hand signals call in a Navy Sea King helicopter to pick up D Squadron's unused equipment one day after the Argentine surrender. Returning home from the South Atlantic, this distinguished SAS unit would revert to its counter-terror role. Within weeks, the troopers would redeploy to Northern Ireland.

from Wireless Ridge, later it became clear that this foray by a handful of men convinced the Argentines that they had interrupted a major landing attempt.

Next morning, Rod Bell resumed his broadcasts, advising the enemy commanders that "the world will judge you accordingly" if there was unnecessary bloodshed. His back to the sea and feeling pressured from two directions by a force he had little intelligence of, General Menendez let it be known that he was prepared to parley. Late in the afternoon of June 14, Bell and the SAS's Mike Rose flew into Port Stanley aboard a Gazelle light helicopter trailing a white flag. Negotiations lasted for two hours, with Rose in constant touch with London via his portable satellite radio.

In the end, Menendez capitulated, and at 9:00 p.m., Marine Major General Jeremy Moore, who had arrived two weeks earlier to take charge of Operation Corporate, accepted the official surrender. Down, after seventy-three days, came the blue-and-white Argentine flag. Aloft soared the Union Jack. ★

Grenada: Tales of Things Gone Wrong

Faces camouflaged, U.S. Army Rangers move off the runway at Point Salines Airport, Grenada, heading toward positions inland. In front, a radio and telephone operator (RTO) packs a PRC-77 radio, its antenna doubled over to make the RTO a less conspicuous target.

The two MC-130E Combat Talon deep-penetration transports had been flying south separately and in radio silence for almost seven hours. Now, as the big Air Force turboprops approached their objective on the evening of October 23, 1983, they joined in loose formation and dropped to a radar-evading 600 feet above the Caribbean Sea. On the flight decks, eerily illuminated in the glow of red cockpit lights, the pilots scanned the Talons' special navigation and night-vision devices. Behind, in the cavernous fuselage of each aircraft, eight men wearing parachutes checked their gear and prepared for action. Each one shouldered nearly a hundred pounds of equipment: a rifle, a pistol, a knife, ammunition, hand grenades, survival gear, inflatable life vests, Chemlite chemical marker lights, night-vision goggles, antitank weapons, and other items considered necessary for the mission. In the middle of the cargo holds, fitted with parachute extraction systems, rested the teams' surface transport: a pair of blunt-nosed twenty-three-foot fiberglass Boston Whaler assault boats with 175-hp outboard motors.

The sixteen men were SEALs. Together with a party of Air Force specialists who would join them below, the U.S. Navy commandos would be the vanguard of the most massive American invasion force since the Inchon landing of the Korean War, more than thirty years earlier: thirteen ships, hundreds of fixed-wing aircraft and helicopters, more than 7,000 men in all.

Ahead, barely punctuating the vastness of the sea, lay their target: the tiny, comma-shaped island of Grenada, a place that until recently had been known solely for its cloves and nutmegs, lush scenery, sunny clime, and placid, touristy lifestyle. But now, because of a rapidly developing situation that jeopardized American lives and threatened the regional balance of power, the U.S. military was going into battle. As matters turned out, for all the assembled

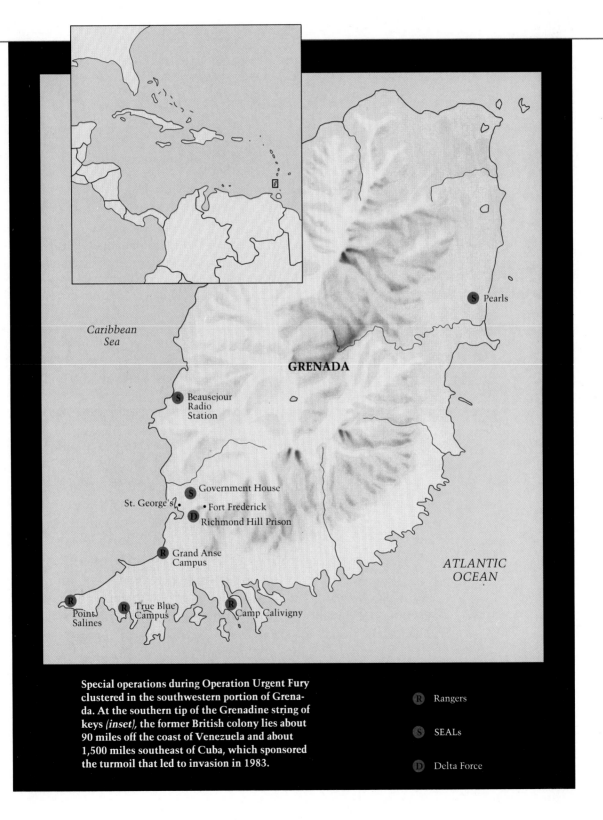

Caribbean
Sea

GRENADA

ⓢ Pearls

ⓢ Beausejour
Radio
Station

ⓢ Government House
St. George's • • Fort Frederick
ⓓ Richmond Hill Prison

ⓡ Grand Anse
Campus

ⓡ Point
Salines

ⓡ True Blue
Campus

ⓡ Camp Calivigny

*ATLANTIC
OCEAN*

**Special operations during Operation Urgent Fury
clustered in the southwestern portion of Grenada. At the southern tip of the Grenadine string of
keys (inset), the former British colony lies about
90 miles off the coast of Venezuela and about
1,500 miles southeast of Cuba, which sponsored
the turmoil that led to invasion in 1983.**

ⓡ Rangers

ⓢ SEALs

ⓓ Delta Force

might, it would be the special-operations forces—the Navy's SEALs, the Army's Delta Force and, above all, its two Ranger battalions—who would bear the brunt of the fighting and dying.

Discovered by Columbus in 1498 during his third voyage to the New World, Grenada is the southernmost island of the Grenadine chain, only ninety miles north of South America. It was a colonial bone of contention for 300 years before finally becoming a British possession, after which the Foreign Office managed affairs until 1974, when the 90,000 Grenadians won independence within the British Commonwealth. But the sweet day of liberty soon turned sour: The first prime minister, one Eric Gairy, proved to be corrupt and heavy-handed, and within five years, he was overthrown by the Marxist New Jewel (Joint Endeavor for Welfare, Education, and Liberation) Movement led by a leftist named Maurice Bishop. The new prime minister was as bad as the first: He clamped a Communist dictatorship on the island and immediately began militarizing Grenada along classic lines, with a People's Revolutionary Army (PRA) and People's Revolutionary Militia (PRM). It did not take long for either Moscow or Havana to see the possibilities.

Fidel Castro, in particular, recognized the advantages of Grenada's strategic location. Cuba at the time was supplying much of the muscle behind the embattled Marxist government of Angola, in Africa, while simultaneously fomenting revolution in Central and South America. Little more than 130 square miles in area, Grenada was minuscule, but it was ideally positioned for both Cuban adventures: as a fueling base for aircraft flying to and from Africa, and as a supply depot and training center for guerrilla and terrorist groups throughout the Caribbean basin and southward.

There was, however, an obstacle to these ambitions: The island had only one airstrip, and it was too short for long-range aircraft. The solution was simple: Hundreds of Cuban construction workers, suspected of having had enough military training to pose a threat, were deployed to begin work on a new "international" airport—for tourism, it was explained—at the southern tip of the island on a narrow spit of land called Point Salines. At the same time, the Grenadian government signed military agreements with Moscow that provided for roughly $20 million worth of arms to be supplied through Cuba. Though the facts were only sketchily

A Grenadian soldier coaches troops from a truck, activity secretly photographed by a civilian who watched the People's Revolutionary Army (PRA) through a three-inch hole that he made in his kitchen wall. Fearful of weapons fired nearby, he also reinforced the wall with a half-inch-thick steel plate.

known at the time, the equipment included BTR-60 and BRDM armored personnel carriers with turret-mounted 12.7-mm heavy machine guns, twin 23-mm ZU-23 antiaircraft cannons, quad 12.7-mm antiaircraft machine guns, 82-mm mortars, and 90-mm recoilless rifles along with thousands of light machine guns, assault rifles, and pistols. With Cuban advisers to match, the fledgling PRA was slated to include a mechanized infantry regiment, two other mobile infantry companies, a ZU-23 antiaircraft company, a mortar platoon, and a reconnaissance company. The PRM was to boast a further five infantry battalions, one ZU-23 company, and two 12.7-mm antiaircraft platoons. By 1982, there were fewer than 5,000 men under arms—with weapons enough for 10,000.

Maurice Bishop became a personal friend of Fidel Castro, visited Hungary and Czechoslovakia, and planned a pilgrimage to Moscow. His stock was riding high in the Communist world. But then, the prime minister fell fatally out of favor with ambitious colleagues who felt that he was not enough of a firebrand revolutionary. On October 14, 1983, he was ousted from office and arrested by Deputy Prime Minister Bernard Coard. Five days later, to ensure the success of the coup, Bishop and nine of his followers were lined up against a wall and sawed into pieces with machine-gun fire; the grisly remains were burned and then buried in a shallow pit. At 9:00 p.m., martial law descended on Grenada.

This brutal and bloody massacre drew immediate world attention. The United States, which had been watching the course of events in Grenada with growing apprehension, was particularly alarmed. An unknown number of young Americans, believed to be in the hundreds, were attending the Saint George's Medical School, an American-owned campus also known as True Blue and located at the southern end of the island. They were now considered to be in harm's way.

A threat to citizens abroad can galvanize any nation, and the United States is no exception. Planning to mount a rescue began in earnest on October 20, the day after Bishop was executed. As the mission evolved, the United States would not only evacuate the students by force; it would also, with the full support of Grenada's neighbors, grasp the opportunity to install a democratic government on the island. As President Ronald Reagan put it at one point during the planning: "Well, if we've got to go there, we might as well do all that needs to be done."

That meant a full-fledged invasion—and with D-day set for the early-morning hours of October 25, there would be only four days to complete the planning for a necessarily large and complex operation. There followed a heroic assembling of military power at a moment's notice. And while it was remarkable that the pieces fit together as well as they did, the flaws were numerous and severe, more than can be ascribed to the fog of war.

Command and control would be a massive problem. Since the invasion was to be an all-service show, the task force was inevitably plagued by units and staffs that had never worked together. They employed different procedures, codes, and radio frequencies, and they made their plans in ignorance of one another. Worse was the virtual absence of U.S. intelligence about Grenada or its armed forces; there was no CIA presence on the island, no recent aerial photos, and only the sketchiest information about Cuban and Grenadian positions, headquarters, and communications and supply centers. Even the location of many of the students was unknown. Moreover, there was an appalling lack of maps with proper military grid coordinates. Units would be going in essentially blind.

Considering Grenada's meteoric rise in profile from quiet backwater to target of an American invasion force, some of these poverties are perhaps understandable; not every point on the globe can get an equal share of intelligence and cartography agencies' limited resources. Nonetheless, the operation—commandos, in particular—would suffer greatly for the deficiencies.

Overall command of the operation, now labeled Urgent Fury, would reside with the Navy's Task Force 120, organized around a carrier battle group, and the 22d Marine Amphibious Unit, designated Task Force 124. The Marines, who had been on their way to Lebanon, were assigned the northern end of the island, with an initial landing near Pearls Airport. Securing the southern half of the island was to be mainly a joint special-operations show. An element of the Navy's SEAL Team Six was to reconnoiter the new airfield abuilding at Point Salines and guide an Air Force combat control team, which would place radio-navigation beacons on the field and direct the swarm of C-130 Hercules transports soon to arrive. On board the Hercs would be two battalions of the 75th Regiment, Army Rangers: the First Battalion from Fort Stewart, Georgia, and its sister unit, the Second Battalion from Fort Lewis, Washington. The black-beret Rangers, highly trained light infantry whose forte is nighttime seizures of airfields, would either parachute in or perform an assault landing to secure the Salines strip. Then, they would race to the nearby True Blue medical campus, where the American students were believed to be.

Meanwhile, other SEALs were to scout around Pearls Airport for the Marines, capture the island's main radio station at Beausejour, and rescue from house arrest Britain's governor general on the island, Sir Paul Scoon. The Army's Delta Force, specializing in hostage rescues, drew the task of releasing political prisoners thought to be held at Richmond Hill Prison. Finally, elements of the 82d Airborne Division were to fly into Salines airfield on board giant C-141 Starlifter transports; relieve the Rangers, SEALs, and Delta operatives; and proceed with whatever mopping up was necessary.

A Reconnaissance Goes Sour

The sixteen men of SEAL Team Six flying in the Combat Talons nearing Grenada on the evening of October 23 had been tapped for the Salines recon effort. They were to arrive off the southern coast of the island, parachute into the sea, climb aboard their Whalers, and rendezvous with the destroyer *Clifton Sprague*. There, they would take on another three SEALs and a trio of Air Force combat

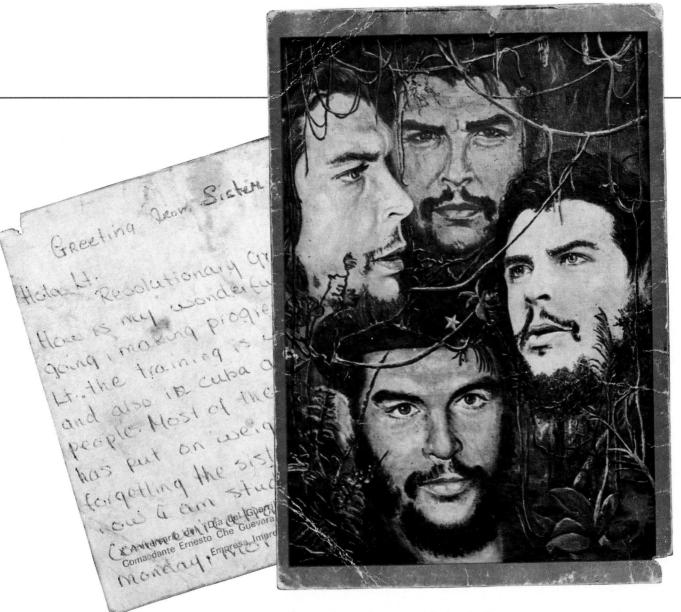

Visages of Cuban revolutionary Ernesto "Che" Guevara adorn a postcard found tacked to the lid of a soldier's footlocker. The message on the back of the card resonates with the enthusiasm of a young woman sent to Cuba for communications training.

controllers. Then they would check their equipment one last time and head for the beach. Once ashore, the group was to check the runway at Salines for obstructions and serviceability, emplace beacons, and hide through the day to await the Rangers' arrival in the early hours of the twenty-fifth. Ordinarily, an Air Force combat control team jumps on or close to its objective, but the location of the Salines strip ruled that out. The runway ran the length of a narrow cape with the sea on three sides. If the parachutists drifted in the wind, they would either alight in the ocean or, more unfortunate still, land in the middle of one of two Cuban compounds on the north side of the runway. The answer was to insert them by sea with SEALs as their guides and guardians.

From start to finish, the mission was a debacle. As the Combat

Talons approached the drop point and the SEALs stood for the jump, the men knew that they already were in trouble. The drop was to have been at dusk, with just enough daylight to see their Boston Whalers. But miscellaneous delays had put them some six hours behind schedule. To parachute into the sea at night is hazardous at best. A jumper can become entangled in shroud lines and canopy. If the wind fills his chute, a man can be dragged facedown across the water and drown. On this night gusts were topping twenty-five knots, a "no-go" in peacetime and well beyond the eighteen-knot limit recommended for combat jumps. The trick to survival was to unlatch the quick-release parachute harness at exactly the right height above the sea—too low and the parachutist risked entanglement, too high and striking the water for the heavily laden SEALs would be like hitting concrete. Yet, height above the water is next to impossible to judge at night.

Inside the MC-130Es, green jump lights flashed on as the planes, now flying level at 2,000 feet for the drop, passed over the *Clifton Sprague.* First the boats, jerked out of the open rears of the airplanes by huge cargo parachutes, then the sixteen men tumbled into the darkness—and disaster.

The commandos had been divided over the wisdom of carrying so much weight into the water; the recommended maximum load is only sixty pounds. Furthermore, there had been no time to conduct the customary "dip test," in which a SEAL jumps fully loaded into the water as a buoyancy check. But the officer in charge, loath to leave any of the equipment behind and fearing that loading any of it into the Whalers might break the boats on impact with the water, argued that they could manage, and his men went along with the idea—some of them reluctantly.

All eight men from the first transport sank into the sea. Five of them surfaced; three did not, presumably drowned. One survivor said later: "I knew damn well we might not make it with all that gear hanging on us. I started dumping everything the minute I got a canopy. I still must have gone to sixty feet when I hit before I could get headed up. When I surfaced, I looked around and began counting Chemlites. I thought we'd lost more than three." The five searched in vain for their Whaler and drifted in their life jackets until after daylight, when they were picked up by a launch from the *Sprague.*

Faring only a little better, the second team lost one of its number. The remaining seven eventually found their Whaler and made it to the *Sprague,* where they linked up with the Air Force combat control team and started out on the recon mission. But as they approached Point Salines near dawn, an enemy patrol boat appeared and they had to abort the attempt. The next night, October 24, the SEALs grimly tried again. Again, a Grenadian patrol boat came on the scene. This time, the SEALs killed their outboard motor, hunkered down, and drifted silently in the darkness. After a harrowing wait, they watched the enemy vessel pass into the night. But when the SEALs tried to restart the outboard, it would not catch. Incredibly, the motor was dead, and now the tide began pulling the SEALs out to sea. They would drift for eleven hours before finally being picked up by the *Sprague.* The Salines-bound Rangers would have no advance information on the condition of the strip or the extent of its defenses.

Other SEALs reconnoitering in advance of the Marine assault had considerably more success. On the night of the twenty-fourth, elements of SEAL Team Four attached to the Marine amphibious unit (MAU) made their way ashore through ten miles of rough water aboard two Seafox raiding boats from the landing ship *Fort Snelling.* The Seafoxes, low-profile, high-speed craft mounting a .50-caliber machine gun and a 40-mm grenade launcher, were each crewed by three members of Special Boat Unit 20, the task force's small-boat detachment specially versed in the support of SEAL operations. By midnight the teams were ashore. One group scouted the coastline while the second made its way inland toward the airport. The beach team quickly determined that a reef and rough surf conditions precluded the use of the Marines' armored amphibious landing vehicles. At 4:00 a.m., they sent a message to the task force's command center on the helicopter assault ship *Guam:* "Walking Track Shoes." The beach was no good.

An assault would have to be made on Pearls Airport by helicopter, even though doing so would deny the invaders armor support. Then more bad news arrived from the team that was scouting the airfield. The men had managed to creep close enough to eavesdrop on Grenadian soldiers and hear mentioned that the defenses included some of the PRA's 23-mm antiaircraft cannons.

Now invasion planners offshore would have to find a substitute landing zone for the Marine CH-46 transport choppers. The site would have to lie beyond the range of these weapons, yet close enough to permit a rapid assault on the airport. H-hour, the jump-off

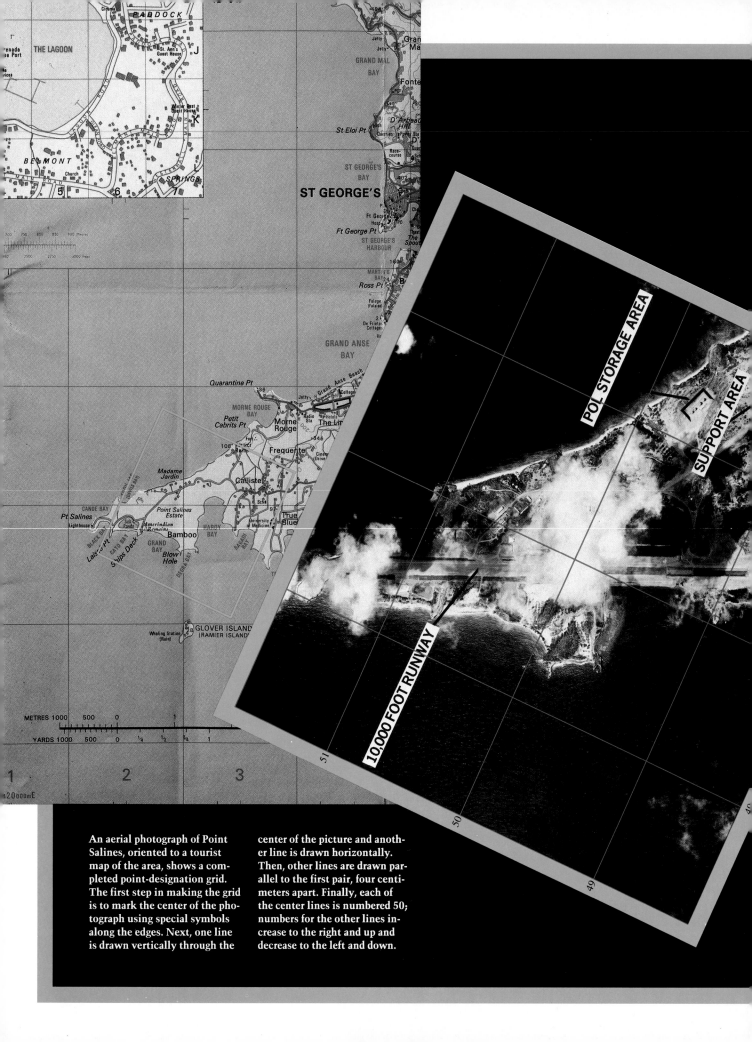

POL STORAGE AREA

SUPPORT AREA

10,000 FOOT RUNWAY

An aerial photograph of Point Salines, oriented to a tourist map of the area, shows a completed point-designation grid. The first step in making the grid is to mark the center of the photograph using special symbols along the edges. Next, one line is drawn vertically through the center of the picture and another line is drawn horizontally. Then, other lines are drawn parallel to the first pair, four centimeters apart. Finally, each of the center lines is numbered 50; numbers for the other lines increase to the right and up and decrease to the left and down.

From Aerial Photo to Map

Although few regions of the world remain uncharted, the maps available for many areas may be so out-of-date that they are next to useless either for special operations or for any other kind of military undertaking. One solution is to use an overhead photograph, taken by satellite or aircraft, either as a substitute for a map when none exists or to supplement an imperfect one.

The first step of turning a picture into a map is to calculate the scale, the ratio of distance on the photograph to distance on the ground. A scale of 1:50,000, for example, means that one inch on the picture equals 50,000 inches (4,167 feet) on the ground. As it happens, scale is also equal to the ratio between the distance from lens to film (focal length) and the distance from lens to ground (aircraft altitude less ground elevation).

Except for elevation, the camera records this data at the instant of exposure. It also notes the coordinates at the center of the picture and the time the photograph was taken. Together with shadows in the picture, the time of day helps establish north. Finally, a grid is drawn on the photograph, each line representing a distance of 1,000 meters or more, depending on the scale of the picture.

Producing a map supplement from a photograph is simpler because the existing map indicates scale and north. All that is needed is a uniform method of drawing a point-designation grid on a photograph and of referring to it. Those procedures, explained here, are taught in various special-operations schools and make it possible for parties that have a copy of the picture to find and discuss a detail in the photograph by citing common grid coordinates.

This technique came in handy for Rangers during the 1983 U.S. invasion of Grenada, when the only maps available were old tourist guides that did not show key objectives, such as the 10,000-foot runway being built at Point Salines by Cuban combat engineers.

Grid coordinates are written as six digits—512497 for the POL storage area in the inset. The first three digits give the horizontal position of the area. Of those, the number on the vertical line to the left of the area yields the first two (51). The third number indicates that the area is two-tenths of the way toward the next vertical line. Reading up the grid in the same way provides the last three numbers of the coordinate, which express the vertical position of the storage site.

time for the invasion, had been set for 5:00 a.m.; less than an hour remained to get the Marines ashore. Aboard the *Guam*, Task Force 120 commander Vice Admiral Joseph Metcalf and his staff had been poring over nautical charts and aerial photographs all night, so they were quickly able to find an abandoned horse-racing track, 700 meters south of the airport, that appeared suitable for a helicopter assault. The first flights of CH-46s took off immediately. Even so, they were twenty minutes behind schedule.

A Costly Improvisation

In evaluating Pearls Airport and the nearby beach as potential landing sites, SEAL Team Four had performed its mission with precision and dispatch, but the Army's Delta Force and other elements of the already ill-fated SEAL Team Six would not do so well. The three-pronged operation in which they were to join was intricate but not beyond men of their caliber. Under cover of darkness and with surprise as their ally, the 100 or so SEALs and Delta Force commandos would sweep in from the sea over southern Grenada aboard nine UH-60 Black Hawk helicopters. One chopper would peel off and deposit SEALs at the Beausejour radio transmitter. Another two would head with their complement of SEALs for the nearby Government House and Sir Paul Scoon, while the remaining six filled with Delta operators would fly on to Richmond Hill Prison.

The helicopter unit was the Army's 160th Special Operations Aviation Battalion, otherwise known as Task Force 160, or the Night Stalkers. But time had been against TF 160 from the start. The alert for an "exercise" had not arrived at Fort Campbell, Kentucky, its home base, until late afternoon on Sunday, October 23. Monday found mechanics scrambling to fold the main-rotor blades of their special long-range UH-60s so that they could be loaded onto three immense C-5A Galaxies for transport to Pope Air Force Base, North Carolina, where they would pick up their passengers.

None of this procedure had been rehearsed with the Air Force crews of the C-5s sent to fetch the helicopters, and none of it went smoothly. Equipment that had been loaded had to be unloaded, rearranged, and then reloaded so that everything fit to the satisfaction of the Air Force loadmasters. Not until 11:00 p.m. did the Galaxies raise their ramps for the flight to Pope.

The Galaxies' ultimate destination was Grantley Adams Airport in Barbados, the field closest to Grenada capable of handling the gigantic planes. By the time the last C-5 touched down at Grantley Adams, it was 3:30 a.m. on the twenty-fifth and H-hour was only ninety minutes away. There was no possibility that the Black Hawks could be unloaded, made ready, and flown the 170 miles to Grenada before daylight. By dint of herculean efforts, the Black Hawks were airborne at 5:30 a.m. and were passing over the *Guam* off Grenada an hour later. But they were ninety minutes late, and the element of surprise had been lost. The sun was up and the enemy alerted; the Marines by now had almost secured Pearls Airport and the First Battalion Rangers were dropping at Salines. One Black Hawk crew, in fact, had tuned in to Grenadian radio, excitedly broadcasting news of the invasion.

As the flight bore inland, one helicopter broke off from the formation and whirled down on the radio station with its tall mast. Within seconds the eight-man assault force was on the ground. A handful of PRA soldiers on guard were quickly captured, and the mission became a matter of holding the station for later use to persuade PRA holdouts to surrender and to calm the populace. The SEAL commander analyzed the terrain. To the west, less than a mile distant, was the ocean. To the south was a river, and near the station to the east was a north-south highway that bridged the river a hundred yards southeast of the station. Across the bridge lay a settlement. Any trouble would arrive by road.

The SEAL commander decided to extend his defenses by deploying two security teams armed with M60 machine guns and M72 light antitank weapons (LAWs) on the road north and south of the station. It was well that he did. The SEALs drew first blood. A truck filled with PRM militiamen, heading south, blundered into the SEAL ambush north of the station. Machine-gun fire laced the air and the truck lurched to a halt in the middle of the kill zone. Five Grenadians were slain, several others were wounded, and the remainder scattered into the bush in panic. The SEALs reloaded and resumed their positions.

Meanwhile, news of the radio station's seizure had reached PRA headquarters at nearby Fort Frederick, and within a few minutes a reaction force led by a Soviet-built BTR-60 armored personnel carrier roared northward to retake the station. The BTR advanced up the road until it came to the bridge—and the other SEAL ambush.

As the shooting began, the PRA soldiers dismounted and started a flanking movement under cover of clattering PKM 7.62-mm light machine guns. The heavier 12.7-mm gun of the personnel carrier punched right through the walls of the radio station and ceased only when a SEAL sent a 66-mm RAW rocket—a developmental anti-armor weapon brought along to test its effectiveness—into the BTR's turret, disabling the gun.

Heavily outnumbered, the commandos were likely to be surrounded before long. The mission was clearly about to fail, and the SEAL commander decided to pull out while he could. If the team reached the beach, the men might be able to swim a mile or two toward the Task Force standing offshore, a comfortable distance for swimmers as fit as SEALs, then signal to be picked up with strobe lights they carried with them as part of the basic SEAL kit.

The SEALs made a dash for it. Two men were lightly wounded in the escape, but all of them reached the beach, slid into the water, and moved along the shoreline until they found a hiding place. After dark, the commandos swam out to sea and turned on their strobe lights. Within minutes, helicopters arrived to hoist them from the sea. As for the radio station, it had already been destroyed by an air strike earlier in the day.

Simultaneously with the action at the radio station, members of SEAL Team Six dispatched to rescue the governor general were experiencing their own embarrassments and frustrations. The pilots of the two Night Stalker Black Hawks carrying the twenty-three-man team, along with three courageous State Department emissaries to Sir Paul Scoon, could not find Government House. The building was clearly visible on the high-altitude overhead photographs used to brief the helicopter crews. From low altitude, however, the mansion was virtually invisible amid the tropical foliage. The choppers circled, looking for the objective, and by the time they spotted it, they had begun taking intense rifle and machine-gun fire from several points outside the walls enclosing Government House.

Ignoring the bullets, the two UH-60s turned toward the intended landing zone. But as they approached, it became apparent that the ground, which had appeared flat in the briefing pictures, was too steep and studded with too many trees to permit landing. Rather than withdrawing, the pilots came to a hover some ninety feet above the ground. As the SEALs fast-roped to earth wearing heavy leather gloves, the enemy fire intensified. The Black Hawks, which

A Nighttime Shock Tactic

Surprise is a force multiplier. In an ambush, for example, it permits a platoon of commandos to take on three or four times their number. Success, however, depends on careful planning followed by iron discipline among the participants.

After reconnaissance, the ambush leader selects his spot, usually along a route that the enemy is known to travel. Criteria for an ambush site include concealment for the ambushers and little cover or maneuver room for the opponent. Terrain should facilitate a stealthy approach to the site and a speedy withdrawal to a prearranged rallying point.

The leader can choose from several types of ambush. To strike an armored column, he may elect to point out targets with lasers and call in air strikes. Or when unacceptably outnumbered, he may detonate a series of claymore mines (page 125), then have his unit melt away without firing a shot. If the odds are more favorable, a line ambush—in which the men are abreast—is the safest; they can fire forward without hitting one another. The L-shaped ambush shown here has the advantage of trapping the enemy in a cross fire. To prevent injury to their own, the commandos plant stakes to limit the swing of their gun barrels.

Most ambushes are set after dark and sprung before dawn. Once in place, the team must remain mute and all but immobile. Insect repellent and even candy, sources of telltale odors, are forbidden. Finally, when the enemy is within the kill zone, the leader fires, touching off a stunning fusillade. If all goes well, the enemy may succumb without firing a shot.

Each man in an L-shaped ambush has a specific assignment. In this case, the leader, positioned near the center of the action, springs the ambush by firing tracers to mark the kill zone *(red)*. Machine gunners *(yellow)* immediately begin firing, as do riflemen *(blue)*. Often doubly armed with grenade launchers, these commandos typically use aiming lights and night-vision gear to shoot at individuals one round at a time. Other riflemen guard the flanks of the position; the radio operator usually watches the rear. After a few seconds, when the enemy can no longer shoot back, the leader calls a cease-fire by shouting or launching a flare into the sky, and the team withdraws.

began taking hits, were driven off, taking with them the three diplomats, the SEALs' second-in-command, and the unit's satellite radio, used to communicate with headquarters on the *Guam.*

Nevertheless, the twenty-two commandos on the ground swiftly disarmed the few frightened policemen on guard and collected the governor general, his family, and his staff. There were fourteen people in all, whom the SEALs gathered in a central room of the mansion to lessen the risk of injury should the Grenadians assault the house. Scoon was in friendly hands, but he was far from safe. Because of the groundfire, an aerial evacuation was out of the question. The SEALs would have to hang on until friendly forces could get through to them.

Barely had the commandos taken defensive positions when the Grenadians launched an attack. A BTR-60 rolled through the main gate and started hammering away at Government House, while two groups of infantry began creeping toward the building to surround it. The SEALs let loose with everything they had: M16 rifles, M60 machine guns, M72 LAW antitank rockets, even a .50-caliber sniper rifle. But they were outnumbered and outgunned. Unless relieved by nightfall, they expected to be overrun.

By means of their short-range squad radios—similar to the handheld units carried by police officers—and a relay set up by other SEALs, the embattled Team Six managed to inform its headquarters of its predicament. Nearly four tense hours later, salvation rumbled overhead in the form of an AC-130 Spectre gunship of the Air Force's Eighth Special Operations Squadron. This awesome weapons system, based on a C-130 Hercules transport, had more firepower than a tank: a battery of 20-mm Vulcan and 40-mm Bofors automatic cannons, and even a 105-mm howitzer capable of firing as many as eight forty-pound shells per minute.

The AC-130 laid down a curtain of 20-mm and 40-mm fire at 10:15 a.m., and subsequently during the day, other Spectres arrived to discourage the PRA. At one point, a Spectre hosed down a group of the enemy trying to penetrate the mansion perimeter. A laconic radio transmission from the aircraft described the results of the brief episode. "I see twenty flappers and kickers," crackled a voice reporting the number of dead and wounded, "and seven runners."

As evening approached, the SEALs requested permission to attempt a breakout. Instead, orders came to stay put until the arrival of a Marine rescue force, which was already on the way. Through

the night, Navy A-7 attack aircraft from the carrier *Independence* ran occasional strafing runs, keeping the Grenadians at bay. The Marines arrived shortly after sunrise. The governor general was safe, and amazingly, considering all the shooting that had gone on, only one SEAL had been wounded. Yet a rescue that was to have been a swift, surgical operation performed in a few minutes had lasted more than twenty-four hours.

After the three SEAL-bearing TF 160 Black Hawks had departed the formation for the radio station and Government House, the remaining six, carrying a total of some sixty Delta Force commandos, had pressed on toward Richmond Hill Prison. As with the other missions, neither the UH-60 pilots nor the Delta operators had received much information in their preraid briefing. They knew the location and general layout of the prison, but they had no knowledge of the surrounding terrain or what enemy defenses might be. The mission concept assumed that the raid would go in before daybreak and catch most of the Grenadians asleep, that defenses would be negligible, that suitable landing zones would present themselves, and that the raiders could easily overwhelm a few bored guards.

The plan was little more than an outline. It called for two UH-60s carrying Delta troopers to close on the prison and for the door gunners to take out the guard towers. The choppers would then land, one on each side of the prison, and discharge a blocking and security force. Simultaneously, the four other helicopters were to race in and hover above the prison yard. The rescue force would then fast-rope to the ground and release everyone who could be found.

Aboard the assault ship *Guam*, a UH-60 Black Hawk gets a shot of water in the air intakes from deck hands trying to shut down the helicopter's engines. The pilot could not stop them, in all likelihood because groundfire during a raid on Government House damaged the chopper's fuel-control system, perhaps jamming a valve open.

There had been no time either to gather the detailed intelligence or to conduct the thorough rehearsal that is essential to a successful rescue effort, but the Delta Force troopers shrugged off the deficiencies. "We thought it was all a walk, a cakewalk," recalled one commando. "So nobody was really jacked about the whole thing." No one seemed to realize that the prison sat on a ridge overlooking a deep valley, its twenty-foot-high walls projecting up from an extremely steep incline overgrown with jungle—or that PRA headquarters was at Fort Frederick, perched only 300 yards across the ravine from the target.

Inside the fort, the alarm sounded as soon as the thudding rotor blades were heard. Almost a company of riflemen armed with AK-47 assault rifles immediately rushed to the ramparts, and antiaircraft gunners climbed into the seats of two ZPU-4 antiaircraft machine guns on the roof. These four-barrel, 14.5-mm weapons fired 600 rounds per minute.

As the six Black Hawks flew along the rising valley floor, Fort Frederick seemed to erupt in fire, and curving green tracer rounds reached down toward the choppers. Almost at once the helicopters started taking hits. Jagged holes appeared in the fuselages of the lead ships, and men started yelling and screaming as the bullets bit into them and blood splattered everywhere. "From the top of those hills where the prison and the fort were just all this green stuff was coming up, crossing all through everywhere," said one of the men. "You could hear the choppers getting hit. Everyone and their brother were taking potshots."

In a desperate attempt to evade the fire from Fort Frederick, the lead ship began twisting and turning. The other pilots matched his every move as best they could without running into the sides of the valley. In the cockpit of the number-four Black Hawk, Captain Keith Lucas, the pilot, was hit in the right arm, and the door gunner, Specialist Loren Richards, took a round in the leg. But Lucas and his copilot, Warrant Officer Paul Price, kept control and managed to follow the others out to sea.

The six aircraft formed up for another try at the prison. Designed from experience gained in Vietnam to absorb punishment and keep on flying, the Black Hawks, though badly hammered, were still airworthy. And the Night Stalker pilots were the cream of U.S. Army aviation—as courageous as they were skilled. Keith Lucas was again fourth into the valley. As his helicopter passed within

Richmond Hill Prison appears here as seen from Fort Frederick, situated on a higher bluff little more than 300 yards away. PRA gunners there had no trouble hitting six helicopters that passed their way early in the fighting on Grenada carrying Delta Force to the prison.

300 yards of Fort Frederick, five rounds exploded through Lucas's windshield. One smashed into his chest and another into his head, killing him instantly. A bullet grazed copilot Price on the head, but he kept control of the bucking, smoking Black Hawk and somehow managed to swing around and start out of the valley. But the helicopter was hit again, and the controls jammed as he fought to clear an onrushing hill.

He almost made it. The UH-60 slammed down onto the crest and skidded along, the fuselage splitting in half, the rotor blades thrashing the ground and breaking away in a shriek of tortured metal. Price struggled out of the cockpit and with some others who had been thrown free started dragging men out of the wreckage before it burst into flame. Miraculously, only Lucas died, but the rest of the men aboard the Black Hawk were either wounded or injured, four of them grievously.

Now, one of the five remaining helicopters came pounding back to provide cover with its door guns. Another UH-60 hovered overhead while nine commandos fast-roped down to administer first aid and help the survivors to the beach below the hill. There they would wait for medevac—and wait and wait. Because of uncoordinated communications between the services, a Navy CH-53 rescue helicopter would not arrive to retrieve the bleeding, broken men for another three and a half hours.

Meanwhile, the four Black Hawks carrying wounded gingerly landed them on the ships offshore (shipboard operations were not in the Night Stalkers' repertoire), then took off for Point Salines with the unhurt Delta Force operators aboard. They expected to find the airfield securely in American hands, but as they approached, they could see perhaps a company of Americans along the south side of the east-west runway exchanging fire with Grenadian defenders who manned

Smoke billows from the wreckage of a
Black Hawk helicopter as a C-130 trans-
port heads for Barbados after ferrying
Rangers to their drop zone at Point Salines
Airport. The Task Force 160 chopper,
piloted by Captain Keith Lucas *(inset)*,
was downed on its second attempt to lift
Delta Force commandos into Richmond
Hill Prison. By the time of the crash,
Lucas was already dead, the victim of
gunshot wounds.

12.7-mm machine guns and ZU-23 rapid-fire cannons on nearby hills northwest of their position. Choosing the least hazardous location to set down, the pilots landed the helicopters at the east end of the runway. Judging them as unfit for further combat, the troops established a security perimeter around their choppers and waited for the invasion to play itself out.

To Parachute or Not to Parachute

The Americans seen from the TF 160 helicopters were Rangers charged with securing the airfield. Like the other special-operations troops, the Rangers had been beset by problems from the start. To begin with, they had no more precise intelligence than anyone else on enemy strength, locations, or fighting ability. Their maps, black-and-white photocopies of an old British tourist guide, were out-of-date and showed nothing of terrain. What is more, a shortage of Air Force C-130 crews qualified for night insertions limited the two battalions to half-strength or less. The 75th Regiment's First Battalion, under Lieutenant Colonel Wesley Taylor, had but 350 of its 700 men; the Second Battalion, under Lieutenant Colonel Ralph Hagler, counted fewer than 250 men. Supporting the understrength battalions would be three of the potent AC-130 Spectres.

Originally, the plan was for Taylor's battalion to go in first. Alpha Company, arriving at Point Salines thirty minutes ahead of the other Rangers aboard two MC-130 Combat Talons, would secure the runway and clear away any obstacles. Then five conventional C-130s would deliver the rest of the First Battalion as two of the AC-130s circled overhead to provide whatever air cover might be needed. Two minutes later, five more C-130s would arrive with Hagler's Second Battalion. With the exception of Taylor's Company A, which would parachute in, the Rangers planned to make an assault landing and taxi swiftly to the end of the runway nearest True Blue. Three gun jeeps carrying up to seven troops apiece would then drive down the loading ramp at the stern of each transport and dash to the students' rescue.

After the SEALs came to grief in their attempts to reconnoiter Salines, it became clear that the Rangers would have to conduct their own reconnaissance from the two MC-130s bearing Alpha Company—plus Colonel Taylor and his command element. When

Screened by a bush, a Delta Force commando mans a security position set up to defend the fleet of eight TF 160 helicopters sitting behind him near the east end of the Point Salines runway. The nearer choppers are four MH-6 Little Birds; they were intended to lift Delta Force to Fort Frederick. The mission was scratched, however, after air defenses at the target proved too strong. Earlier they had so damaged the four Black Hawks in the distance that they were of no further use in the war.

the planes reached Point Salines, a dismaying picture appeared on the scopes of their forward-looking infrared night-vision equipment. Bulldozers, heavy vehicles, and oil drums cluttered the runway. Other debris was scattered everywhere. The time was 4:00 a.m. and to Colonel Taylor in the lead MC-130, it was clear that the Rangers would all have to jump; there was no way that First Battalion's Alpha Company could clear the runway obstacles by the 5:00 a.m. deadline. Taylor radioed the change in plans to the ten C-130s carrying the other 500 Rangers.

But now, the pilot of the lead Combat Talon reported that his navigation equipment was malfunctioning; he was not sure that he could pinpoint the drop zone in the dark. H-hour was postponed to first light—5:30 a.m.—an hour that would let the pilots find the target while giving Grenadian antiaircraft gunners as little help as possible in seeing the planes.

At 5:31, the lead aircraft lined up with the runway, rapidly descending toward the drop altitude of 500 feet, the lowest combat jump since World War II. Just then a searchlight from Point Salines stabbed through the sky and locked onto the first ship, carrying Taylor, his headquarters group, and a single platoon of Rangers. Antiaircraft guns instantly opened up, sending tracers arcing toward the Hercules. Still, the pilot bore on. One minute later, the

Arcs centered on rectangles drawn around gun symbols indicate fields of fire for southwestern Grenada's antiaircraft defenses. Drawn shortly before the invasion by Lieutenant Cecil Prime, chief of artillery of the People's Revolutionary Army, the larger arcs show the range of 23-mm cannons; smaller ones indicate the reach of 12.7-mm machine guns. Among other symbols on the map are black triangles representing observation posts. A large arrow pointing at Saint George's and boat symbols off Grand Anse and Point Salines mark areas where amphibious landings were expected.

SIGNALS AND COMMAND	INDICATION
PREPARE FOR MARCH	707
CARRY OUT MANOEUVRE TOWARDS RESERVE	500
CONTINUE MARCH	100
STOP AND EMPLACE	ARRAW
OCCUPY FIRE POSITION IN	111
MOVE A PLATOON TO	350
REALISE FIRE AGAINST GROUND TARGET	600
REDUCE WASTAGE OF AMMUNITION	700
REPORT YOUR SITUATION	RED
ATTENTION - RELEIVE ORDER	LIGHTENING

green light came on in the troop compartment and the heavily loaded Rangers barreled through the door. Within seconds, the first men hit the ground. But the pilot of the second MC-130, seeing the deadly fireworks ahead, aborted the run and banked away to allow the accompanying Spectre gunships to soften up the defenses on the ground. Taylor and his handful of Rangers—forty-two men in all—were alone on the ground.

As Taylor consolidated what little position he had and his lone platoon began clearing the runway of obstacles—even hot-wiring a bulldozer, which the Rangers then used to flatten steel spikes that had been driven into the tarmac to puncture aircraft tires—the two AC-130s bore down on the ZU-23s and 12.7-mm antiaircraft batteries north and east of the runway. Streams of fire laced the ground, and the antiaircraft guns fell silent. At 5:52 a.m., the second MC-130, carrying the rest of Alpha Company, motored low overhead and made its drop.

The C-130s carrying the rest of the Ranger contingent were by now orbiting at sea, waiting for word to commence their runs into the drop zone. The planes had been in the air for roughly nine hours. On board the droning aircraft, the Rangers, like soldiers everywhere, had grabbed the chance for precious rest on the flight south from Hunter Army Airfield, Georgia. "It's strange," said one Ranger of the ability to sleep under such circumstances. "It's kind of a conditioned response you get after a while. Anyway, with all that tension, everyone went right to sleep. The plane was dead." Men sprawled everywhere around the darkened fuselages—against each other, on piles of parachutes, in the gun jeeps.

Upon learning of the obstructed runway at Point Salines, the officers roused the troops. They had only an hour to prepare for a jump. Cursing and sweating, the Rangers scrambled to don parachutes, repack their rucksacks with ammunition and equipment that had been strapped to the gun jeeps, and check each other out on the buddy system. Within forty-five minutes, seven of the ten Hercules were rigged for the drop: two of Taylor's five conventional C-130s, plus Hagler's five.

Inexplicably, prompt word of the changed plans failed to reach Taylor's other transports. The frantic rush to rerig that resulted from the delay was one to try men's souls. On one of the planes, the Ranger in charge had his men don their chutes. We "started passing out the parachutes," recalled one participant, "started loading up our rucksacks, then it was no, we were going to land. Started putting the crap on the jeeps again." And then, incredibly, the crew chief stuck his head into the hold again and hollered: "Rangers are fighting. Jump in twenty minutes."

"At that point," said the Ranger, "we actually got the parachutes on and got rigged up. We stayed rigged up forever. It was miserable. When you stand hooked up, you have your rucksack across your legs, and those things are ungodly heavy. They just keep pulling you down, and everybody was leaning and laying on stuff and moaning." His own load, besides his rifle: two 60-mm mortar rounds, one LAW rocket, 300 rounds of M60 machine-gun ammunition, one claymore mine, four bandoleers of M16 ammunition, a saline solution IV, two canteens of water, and eighteen hand grenades.

The complaining, however, came to a halt as one of the platoon leaders shouted to the men the news of the intense groundfire at Point Salines. "Kind of perked everyone up when they started giving out these situation reports, kind of an adrenaline rush," remembered the trooper. "Shortly afterwards, the jump doors were open, and the green light came on, and all that fatigue was just gone. Everybody just skipped on out of that bird." It was almost 7:00 a.m.

By 7:05 a.m., the remainder of Taylor's battalion was on the ground. Five minutes later, the men of Hagler's Second Battalion joined them. Thus by 7:10 all the Rangers—save a few jeep drivers still aboard the C-130s, which would land when the runway had been cleared—were at last ready to go to work.

Scattered around the airstrip, the troops were taking sporadic fire from all directions. However, the greatest volume seemed to be coming from Calliste, a settlement 250 yards north of the east end of the runway. Covered by fire from M60 machine guns and 60-mm mortars, a pair of Ranger platoons charged across the tarmac to eliminate that threat, while two full companies closed in on the construction camps half a mile northwest of the runway, where the Cuban airfield workers were thought to be. Meanwhile, other Rangers secured the western end of the airfield and pushed on to rescue the students at True Blue.

The young Americans had been watching in awe since daybreak. "I saw the paratroopers jumping," said one twenty-two-year-old. "It was really thrilling to see, kind of like an old John Wayne movie, but I knew people were going to get killed." When the shooting started, the students immediately dived for cover—under beds, into bathtubs, anywhere that promised protection. Just after 7:30 that morning, the first Ranger element entered the medical school campus. There was a brief exchange of shots at the main gate as PRA guards put up a token resistance. But within a few minutes, the campus was in American hands.

At last, matters seemed to be under control. However, there was a surprise in store for the Rangers. The students at True Blue were anxious to know about their friends at Grand Anse, another campus and housing area on the west coast of the island. Grand Anse? The Rangers had heard nothing whatsoever about that. More than 200 Americans were over there, said the students, and something had to be done to rescue them.

In the meantime, the fight at the airfield was heating up. As the Rangers assaulted Calliste, a PRA 12.7-mm heavy machine gun started pounding away, and the troopers unleashed a hail of fire from their rifles, machine guns, and mortars. A Ranger called out through a bullhorn for the defenders to surrender; the only reply was a burst of fire. At that, another Ranger mounted a captured bulldozer, elevated the blade as a shield, and with his comrades following close behind, advanced clanking and squeaking toward the gun position. The firing ceased, and when they reached the gun, they found it abandoned. One Ranger had been killed in the skirmish, but no one else received a serious wound.

As for the Cubans, they had scarcely fired on the Americans during the parachute drops and even later; it would be discovered after the fighting ended that Castro had ordered them to shoot only in self-defense. But as the Rangers advanced out of the airfield, the Cubans, apparently considering themselves to be under attack, commenced a heavy fire. Nevertheless, both Cuban camps were overrun in short order, with one Cuban killed, twenty-two taken prisoner, and an unknown number having fled into the hills. (Eventually, two dozen Cubans would be killed and 661 would be rounded up for deportation.) The Rangers counted eight dead; a score of men suffered minor wounds.

At around 11:00 a.m., the runway was clear enough for the C-130s to land with the gun jeeps, and the Hercules pilots slapped down in ultrashort assault landings. The Rangers were impressed. "They came in and they were reversing their props immediately and slamming on the brakes. There was just blue smoke and squealing," recalled a trooper. "Then they were whipping around and those gun

jeeps were rolling out the back and they were revving their engines. As soon as those damn jeeps were off, the tailgate was coming up and the guy would release his brakes and take off. They weren't even on the ground for two minutes."

The commander of one of the gun jeeps, Sergeant Randy Cline, was given a mission to secure a road junction 200 yards north of the True Blue campus. Speeding along the dusty tracks, Cline and his four-man crew somehow overlooked the low-lying campus and continued for a bit more than a mile before they realized their error. Turning around, they were hurrying back down the road when they ran into a PRA ambush 900 yards short of safety. The PRA let go at close range. The Rangers fired back with their M60 machine gun. But it was over in seconds; Sergeant Cline and three of his men were slain; one wounded Ranger stumbled back to Salines on foot. Those four men, along with the trooper killed in the attack on Calliste, were the only Rangers lost to enemy action on Grenada.

By midafternoon, the Rangers were in complete control of the airfield and its environs. Yet the Grenadians were not quite finished. Later that day, three BTR-60s accelerated up a road toward the western end of the airstrip and began firing their turret-mounted 12.7-mm machine guns. That was a mistake. The Rangers answered with everything they had: 90-mm recoilless rifles spat armor-penetrating missiles designed for targets much heavier than armored personnel carriers. The lead BTR attempted to turn away but succeeded only in slamming into the second. Both were smothered by fire; the roof hatches flew open and the crews fled, leaving behind two comrades dead in the blazing wreckage. The third BTR got itself turned around but then took a round in the rear. An AC-130 Spectre orbiting overhead finished off the BTR.

By two o'clock, the lead elements of the 82d Airborne Division were landing at Salines and the special-operations role in the invasion was winding down. There were just two more missions, both of them the next day. In the late afternoon of October 26, nine Marine CH-46 Sea Knight helicopters, accompanied by four huge CH-53 Sea Stallions, raced north along the west coast of the island from Salines toward the seaside campus of Grand Anse. Aboard the Sea Knights were elements of Hagler's Second Ranger Battalion totaling 150 men. The Sea Stallions, flying empty and each capable of packing in as many as forty students, would make two trips to evacuate the 233 Americans still stranded at the campus.

For once the operation enjoyed a little current intelligence. The medical school staff and students at True Blue were in telephone contact with their colleagues at Grand Anse, and the U.S. command had been able to develop a thorough plan. The Rangers learned from the Americans they were about to liberate that an enemy position—at the Grenadian Police Training College—bordered the north edge of the campus and that a 12.7-mm antiaircraft gun was emplaced there. On the eastern edge stood a line of houses known as Carifta Cottages and believed to be occupied by PRA soldiers. Both posed a threat and would have to be neutralized. A strike by Navy A-7 Corsair fighter-bombers from the USS *Independence* would deal with the Police Training College and antiaircraft gun, while an AC-130 Spectre would suppress any hostile activity originating from the cottages and provide overall fire support for the Rangers. In addition, a pair of Marine Cobra helicopter gunships, armed with rockets and 20-mm cannons, would make an appearance.

At Grand Anse, students and staff gathered in central dormitories after marking the roofs for the attack pilots with white sheets and covering the windows with mattresses to protect against flying glass. They all wore white armbands for identification and flattened themselves on the floor to await the Rangers.

Precisely at 4:00 p.m., the A-7s screamed in from the sea, and the Spectre and Cobras began working over their objectives. Three minutes later, the nine CH-46 Sea Knights hit the beach in flights of three. The first flight missed its mark by 500 meters, landing south of the school, but the remaining two were on target. Two CH-46s were damaged when their main rotors struck palm trees. Both landed safely, and one, after an evaluation by the crew chief, was restarted and flown to Salines. However, the other had to be abandoned on the beach. Rangers poured out of all the machines and raced for the dormitories, and within half an hour, the students had been rushed to the waiting CH-53 Sea Stallions—all of which had landed safely—herded aboard, and evacuated.

One final objective remained for the Rangers. Camp Calivigny, the main PRA training base atop a seacoast promontory five miles east of Salines, was still intact. Though there had been no ground recon, aerial photos indicated a well laid out installation of about four and a half acres, probably heavily defended. Intelligence briefers suggested that there might be as many as 600 Cubans and thirty Soviet advisers there. It sounded bad, and the 220 men of the

First and Second Battalions assigned to the assault were apprehensive. "We all thought it was a suicide mission," said one of their Black Hawk helicopter pilots. One problem was that the low-angle reconnaissance pictures of the camp, taken from a considerable distance, offered no opportunity to select landing zones.

To make matters worse, the softening-up fire at 4:00 p.m. the next afternoon was farcical. Offshore, the destroyer *Caron* boomed out with its two five-inch guns but inflicted little damage. At the same time, three batteries—seventeen guns—of 82d Airborne 105-mm howitzers fired no fewer than 500 shells at Camp Calivigny. However, misplotting of the artillery battery positions, inaccurate coordinates for Camp Calivigny, and the absence of a forward spotter caused all but one of the shells to splash harmlessly into the sea short of the camp.

A follow-up bombardment by Navy A-7s and an Air Force Spectre leveled the camp, however, and then it was time for the Black Hawks carrying the two companies of Rangers. As the last bomb fell, the helicopters, which had been orbiting offshore, turned toward the coastline and raced in low, skimming the surface of the sea to avoid whatever groundfire the PRA might send up. At the last second, the first four UH-60s popped up over the rim of a 150-foot cliff that fell away from the target on three sides. To the pilots' discomfort, the camp was closer to the cliffs than they had imagined, leaving little room for the helicopters to set down.

The pilot of the first machine managed to land safely on the south edge of the camp and his Rangers darted into the ruins. But the second and third Black Hawks, coming in fast and overshooting the first, flared for a landing inside the compound. As the second machine's wheels touched down and its complement of Rangers piled out, the third, following close behind, began experiencing difficulties. Reports vary from "pilot error" to damage inflicted by groundfire, but for whatever reason, the pilot lost control. His aircraft began to tilt and spin, then pitched into the second machine. Close behind, a fourth Black Hawk pilot maneuvered desperately to avoid the melee before him. He managed to land, but the ground was uneven, and unknown to the pilot, his tail rotor had sustained damage. He attempted to lift

At the Grand Anse Medical School, a Ranger and a white-helmeted crewman from a Marine helicopter guard the beach *(top)* as American students sprint toward a pair of CH-53 Sea Stallions *(middle)*. At bottom, two Marines have lowered the chopper's tailgate to allow the students to board, while a Ranger, crouching in the surf, covers the evacuation.

off again, but the aircraft began to spin. Now out of control, it crashed next to the first two. Within twenty seconds, three UH-60s had been destroyed. Flailing rotor blades had killed three Rangers and injured four others.

Fortunately, only one Cuban was discovered in the camp. He managed to wound two Rangers with an AK-47 before being slain. As a Ranger platoon leader summed up the action: "We didn't find anything worth shooting at."

In war, the success of an operation is its own validation. By that measure, Operation Urgent Fury amounted to a considerable victory. The governor general and 662 American citizens had been rescued without a single death or serious injury among them. An unquestionably brutal regime had been eliminated, much to the delight of most Grenadians, and a destabilizing Cuban adventure in the Caribbean had been nipped in the bud. Moreover, for the United States simply to mount and execute such a complex operation on four days' notice was a triumph.

Yet there was much to be learned, particularly in the way special-

operations units had performed. In the months to come, all the failures of command and control, of procedures and logistics would come under intense scrutiny. Perhaps the main lesson of Grenada would be a better understanding of the nature of special operations. Almost by definition, they were delicate and highly complex. They could not be rushed; they required time to plan, time to practice, time to reconsider and replan and practice again. Above all, success at low cost demanded detailed, up-to-the-minute intelligence, for only the foolhardy would expose relatively few men to an intensely hostile environment without precise information about the enemy.

All of this would be put to study, and next time the call came, the U.S. special-operations units—Special Forces, Rangers, Delta Force, and SEALs—would have a better time of it. ✯

The Art of
Blowing Things Up

A frequent mission of special-operations troops is to blow something up. Many targets—fuel drums *(right)* or planes sitting on an airfield, for example—demand little skill; a good-sized bang will do the job. But tougher targets—such as a bridge, perhaps, or a train—require special training in the selection and placement of explosives to ensure that the objective is met. Responsibility for success lies chiefly with commandos specially trained in demolitions.

As shown on the following pages, there is a great variety of demolition charges and of ways of setting them off. All of the variations make use of chemical compounds that burn with extraordinary speed. In doing so, they release prodigious amounts of heat and gas, resulting in a shock wave called blast. This force tends to emanate equally in all directions but can be strengthened along one axis by adjusting the shape of the charge *(below)*. Tamping—covering one side of a charge with sandbags, rocks, or a heavy casing—tends to strengthen a blast in the direction away from the tamping material.

The most common military explosive is trinitrotoluene, or TNT. Sold commercially as dynamite, it was invented in 1863 by Alfred Nobel. TNT burns at 22,500 feet per second. The higher this rate of detonation (ROD), the greater the shattering effect. Nobel's invention is arbitrarily assigned a relative effectiveness (RE) of 1.00. Other common military explosives include a mixture called RDX, the most powerful nonnuclear explosive known, with an ROD of 28,000 feet per second and an RE of 1.60. Another is called PETN (ROD: 26,000 feet per second; RE: 1.45). These concoctions do not detonate easily. Setting them off requires just the right approach—a chain of lesser explosions leading to the main event. Even so, these materials get a great deal of respect from those who work with them. One inattentive moment, and the perpetrator can become the victim.

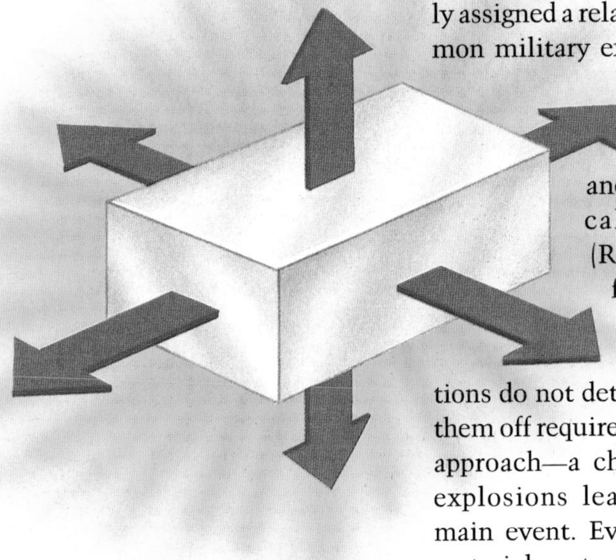

A basic theory. Blast in an explosion results from a kind of flash fire that, in microseconds, changes a small volume of a solid into a huge volume of intensely hot, high-pressure gas. As shown below for a simple block of explosive, the force radiates outward equally and at right angles to every surface of the charge.

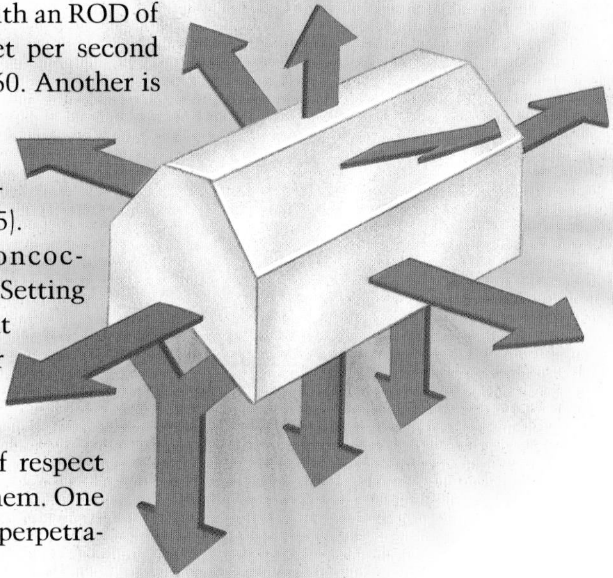

Effects of shape. The omnidirectional nature of an explosion can be altered by contouring the charge. Forces from the sides of a channel molded into the bottom of a block of explosive, for example, meet at the center of the groove *(below)*, packing a greater punch than those from a similar block having a flat bottom. Trimming the corners reduces unwanted backblast.

A Chemical Chain of Events

Tools for Demolition

Of the chemical explosives available, the ones used by the armed forces are composed of TNT or RDX mixed with other ingredients to make them malleable or less concentrated. Virtues of the most common concoctions appear at far right. While each has preferred uses, they all have one thing in common: For safety, they are surprisingly stable and rarely explode unless set off by a detonator.

Often called blasting caps, detonators are designed to be activated either by a fuze, or detonating cord, or by electrical impulse. In either case, the sequence—including the detonator—that leads to the main explosive charge is known as a firing train.

The first component of a firing train is called an initiator, the device that sets in motion a chain of events that ends in the detonation of the main charge. The initiator is connected to a conductor, either something that burns or a wire that conducts an electrical pulse. The fuze or wire leads to a blasting cap, which must be slipped into a well in the main charge to set it off. In some instances, the detonator can simply be pressed into the explosive like a stick into modeling clay. Components of chemical firing trains appear at right. Parts for the electrical version, often chosen for its dependability, are shown on the next page.

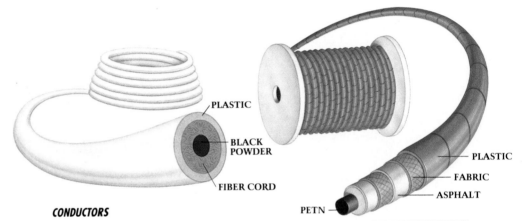

TWO INITIATORS

The heart of a mechanical initiator is a percussion cap filled with a small amount of an explosive so unstable that it can be set off by a blow from a spring-loaded firing pin. In an instant-action initiator (above, left), a tug on a ring (after removing a safety pin) pulls back the firing pin and releases it. A time-delay pencil (above, right) contains an acid-filled glass ampule. Finger pressure crushes the vial, releasing the acid to dissolve a wire that restrains the firing pin. An ampule of weak acid postpones firing up to five hours or more, depending on temperature; stronger acid shortens the delay to less than five minutes.

CONDUCTORS

Chemical conductors come in two varieties, delayed-action fuze (above, left) and instant-firing detonating cord (above, right). Fuze consists of a plastic tube with a core of black powder, which burns at the rate of a foot every thirty to forty-five seconds and can be used with either type of initiator. Detonating cord has a core composed of an explosive that is too stable for a percussion cap to set off. This conductor is detonated either by fuze or by blasting cap (below).

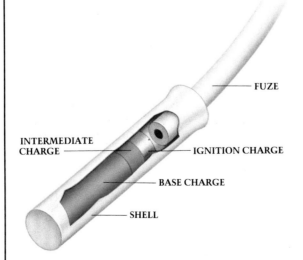

A BLASTING CAP

A fuze-activated blasting cap consists of three charges in an aluminum shell. An ignition charge, lit by a fuze, sets off an intermediate charge. Instantly, this blast ignites a high-explosive base charge that activates the main charge. Blasting caps must be handled with care; the ignition charge is so sensitive that it can be set off by impact.

Jump-Starting an Explosion

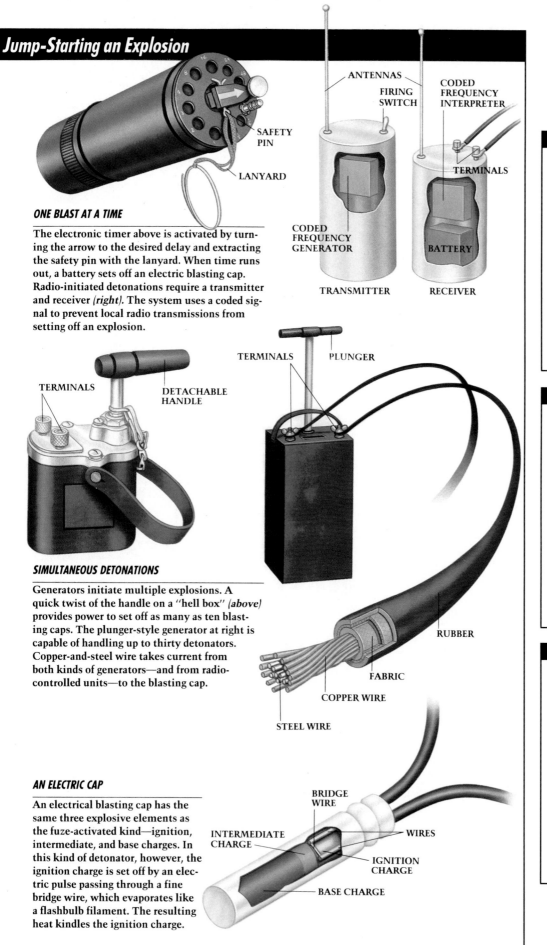

ANTENNAS

FIRING SWITCH

CODED FREQUENCY INTERPRETER

SAFETY PIN

LANYARD

TERMINALS

CODED FREQUENCY GENERATOR

BATTERY

TRANSMITTER

RECEIVER

ONE BLAST AT A TIME

The electronic timer above is activated by turning the arrow to the desired delay and extracting the safety pin with the lanyard. When time runs out, a battery sets off an electric blasting cap. Radio-initiated detonations require a transmitter and receiver *(right)*. The system uses a coded signal to prevent local radio transmissions from setting off an explosion.

TERMINALS

DETACHABLE HANDLE

TERMINALS   PLUNGER

SIMULTANEOUS DETONATIONS

Generators initiate multiple explosions. A quick twist of the handle on a "hell box" *(above)* provides power to set off as many as ten blasting caps. The plunger-style generator at right is capable of handling up to thirty detonators. Copper-and-steel wire takes current from both kinds of generators—and from radio-controlled units—to the blasting cap.

RUBBER

FABRIC

COPPER WIRE

STEEL WIRE

AN ELECTRIC CAP

An electrical blasting cap has the same three explosive elements as the fuze-activated kind—ignition, intermediate, and base charges. In this kind of detonator, however, the ignition charge is set off by an electric pulse passing through a fine bridge wire, which evaporates like a flashbulb filament. The resulting heat kindles the ignition charge.

BRIDGE WIRE

INTERMEDIATE CHARGE

WIRES

IGNITION CHARGE

BASE CHARGE

C-4

An improvement on a compound developed by the British in World War II, C-4 is also called plastique. It is made of TNT combined with other compounds that give it the elasticity of modeling clay and an RE of 1.26. The water-resistant white explosive is highly stable. It can be hurled, crushed, pounded—even burned as a cooking fuel—without risk of explosion.

A-3

Composition A-3 (RE 1.35) is a mixture of 91 percent RDX with 9 percent wax added as a binder and to stabilize the compound. Though more powerful than C-4, it is comparatively brittle and consequently less versatile than plastique. Like C-4, it is largely unaffected by water and is frequently selected for underwater demolitions.

HBX-1

Slate gray HBX-1 (RE 1.48) is a combination of RDX and TNT mixed with aluminum powder to promote burning—plus stabilizing ingredients. Fully waterproof, HBX-1 (and a close cousin called HBX-3) are ideal for use underwater. Consequently, these mixtures often serve as the explosive charge in limpet mines *(pages 108-109)*, torpedoes, and other naval ordnance.

A High-Powered Bag of Explosives

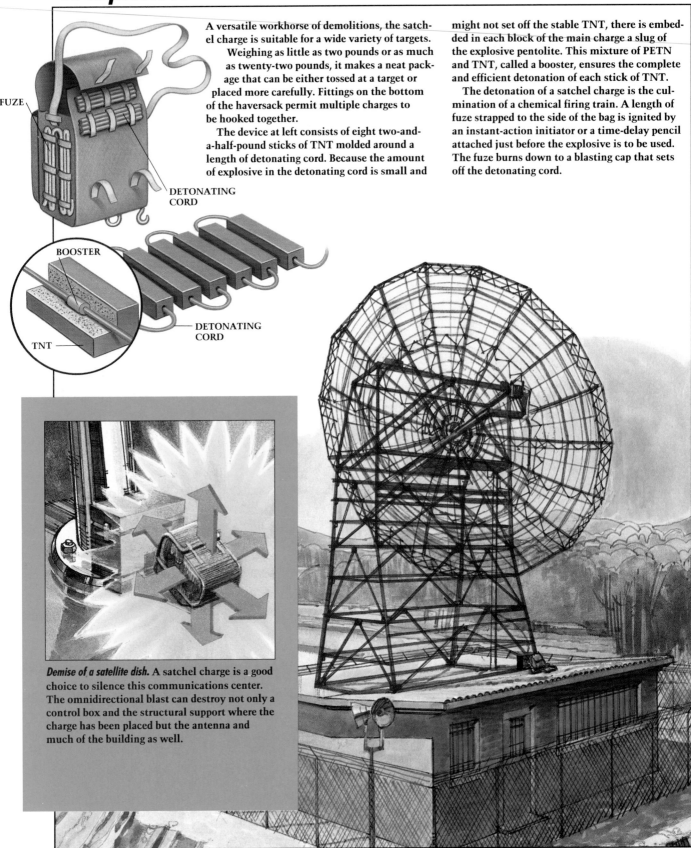

A versatile workhorse of demolitions, the satchel charge is suitable for a wide variety of targets.

Weighing as little as two pounds or as much as twenty-two pounds, it makes a neat package that can be either tossed at a target or placed more carefully. Fittings on the bottom of the haversack permit multiple charges to be hooked together.

The device at left consists of eight two-and-a-half-pound sticks of TNT molded around a length of detonating cord. Because the amount of explosive in the detonating cord is small and might not set off the stable TNT, there is embedded in each block of the main charge a slug of the explosive pentolite. This mixture of PETN and TNT, called a booster, ensures the complete and efficient detonation of each stick of TNT.

The detonation of a satchel charge is the culmination of a chemical firing train. A length of fuze strapped to the side of the bag is ignited by an instant-action initiator or a time-delay pencil attached just before the explosive is to be used. The fuze burns down to a blasting cap that sets off the detonating cord.

FUZE

DETONATING CORD

BOOSTER

DETONATING CORD

TNT

Demise of a satellite dish. A satchel charge is a good choice to silence this communications center. The omnidirectional blast can destroy not only a control box and the structural support where the charge has been placed but the antenna and much of the building as well.

A Sinuous Path of Destruction

Flexible enough to be wrapped around or draped across irregular targets, the snakelike line charge is suitable for blowing a path through natural barriers such as reefs and sand bars. The model shown here, the Mark 8 flexible linear demolition charge, comes in twenty-five-foot lengths of two-inch-diameter rubber hose, each containing fifty pounds of a mix that is 70 percent A-3 explosive and 30 percent aluminum powder. At either end of the charge is a TNT booster.

Line charges screw together, permitting several of them to be linked. A cap with a towing ring is fitted to one end of the assembly to help maneuver it into position. The cap for the other end has a hole through which detonating cord is threaded and knotted so it will not pull out. Screwed tightly to the line charge, this cap holds the detonating-cord knot firmly against a blasting cap that sets off the first TNT booster, getting the explosion under way.

TOW RING

MAIN CHARGE

BLASTING CAP

DETONATING CORD

THREADED COUPLINGS

BOOSTER

Leveling an underwater obstacle. Dipping and rising with the contours of a coral reef, a multisection line charge is arranged serpentine-fashion, as shown above, or in a crisscross grid pattern. Exploding in all directions at once, it opens a wide breach in the reef that allows landing craft or other shallow-draft vessels to pass. For ocean-bottom explosions like this, detonating cord is usually run ashore or to a boat on the surface and then set off either by fuze or with a timer.

The Penetrating Effect of a Shaped Charge

Unfocused blast such as that produced by satchel and line charges *(pages 102-103)* requires a sometimes-impractical amount of explosives to destroy structures built of thick steel or concrete. Indeed, these materials can act as a form of tamping, directing the force of the explosion away from the target.

The answer is a shaped charge like the one below. Its cylindrical explosive has a conical hollow in one end that directs most of the blast toward the base of the cone. A glass liner forms a molten slug that can penetrate thirty-six inches into concrete and twelve inches into steel. For thicker targets, a second charge can be laid in the cavity made by the first—after the glass slug is shattered with a hammer and disposed of.

Where a demolition team can gain access to opposite sides of a structure (bridge supports are a good example) two shaped charges can be used to make an "earmuff" charge. To ensure that the earmuffs explode simultaneously, they are linked with detonating cord, which is set off by another length of the same material knotted at the midpoint of the link. Joined by more detonating cord, several earmuff charges can be set off at the same time. To knock out the bridge at right, the charges are attached with claylike adhesive opposite each other on supports that span the length of one side. This approach will either topple the bridge or weaken it so much as to make it unusable, especially by trucks or other heavy vehicles.

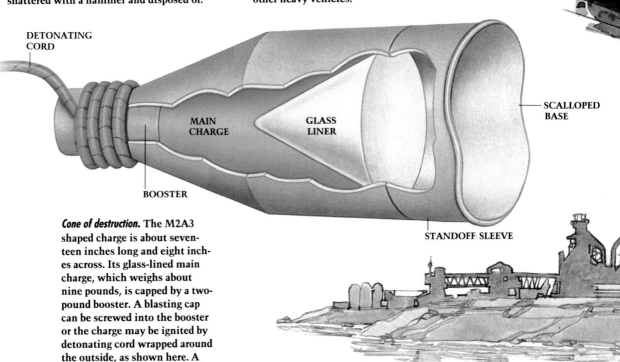

DETONATING CORD

MAIN CHARGE

GLASS LINER

SCALLOPED BASE

BOOSTER

STANDOFF SLEEVE

Cone of destruction. The M2A3 shaped charge is about seventeen inches long and eight inches across. Its glass-lined main charge, which weighs about nine pounds, is capped by a two-pound booster. A blasting cap can be screwed into the booster or the charge may be ignited by detonating cord wrapped around the outside, as shown here. A standoff sleeve, scalloped at the edge to help adapt the charge to irregular surfaces, holds the explosive at the optimum distance for greatest penetration.

When earmuffs explode. Shock waves from two shaped charges detonated simultaneously on opposite sides of a concrete bridge piling collide inside the structure and then rebound. Not flexible enough to absorb the sudden reversal, the concrete crumbles.

Slicing Steel Beams with C Charges

To sever something—a tree trunk, perhaps, or a steel girder—demolitions specialists fashion a cutting charge from a malleable explosive such as C-4. If intelligence about the target is accurate and detailed, the charges may be prepared before the mission. Otherwise, the explosive is prepared at the scene.

Custom-fabricated charges like these make it easy to use two independent firing trains, in this case detonating cord and a pair of blasting caps. This redundancy reduces the chance of a misfire. If, for example, the probability of firing-train failure is one in ten, then using two trains reduc-es the likelihood of a dud to one in a hundred.

To knock down a structure made of steel girders, multiple charges are often needed. For example, toppling the radio mast at right, which is built of steel less than two inches thick, demands a cutting charge at each corner, two placed high and two low. (Thicker beams require two charges placed opposite each other.) When the explosives detonate, cutting the girders, the tower will fall in the direction of the lower charges, easily snapping guy wires that depend on the structural integrity of the tower for their ability to keep it standing in high winds.

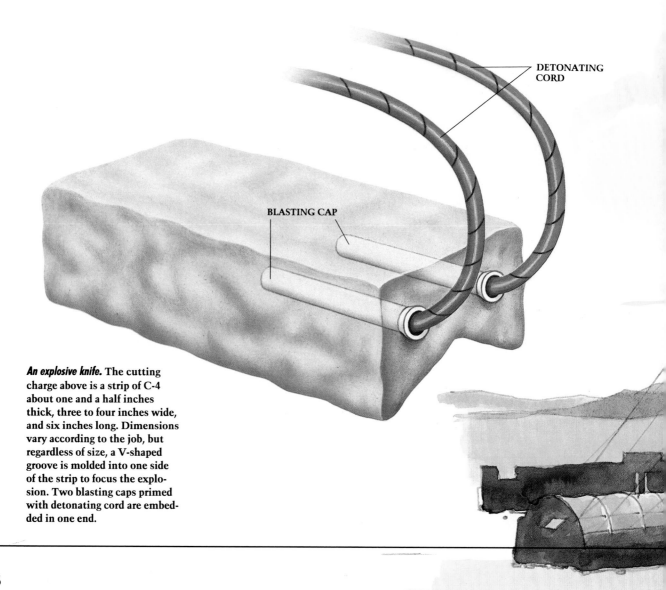

DETONATING CORD

BLASTING CAP

An explosive knife. The cutting charge above is a strip of C-4 about one and a half inches thick, three to four inches wide, and six inches long. Dimensions vary according to the job, but regardless of size, a V-shaped groove is molded into one side of the strip to focus the explosion. Two blasting caps primed with detonating cord are embedded in one end.

Fitting the shape to the target. To sever a girder, a cutting charge is bent to slip between its flanges. A block of wood tamps the charge, increasing the amount of blast directed toward cutting the beam. In this case, a blasting cap is pressed into each end of the charge to make the explosion as uniform as possible. Lashings *(not shown)* hold the charge in position.

A Hull-Gripping Mine That Destroys Ships

C-4, A-3, and other explosives can be used against underwater targets. However, after twelve hours or so of submersion, these materials become so waterlogged that they will not detonate. Thus, demolitions teams attacking a ship below the water line will almost always choose a waterproof explosive such as HBX-3, often in the form of a limpet mine. Named for the mollusk that clings tenaciously to undersea rocks, limpet mines are attached to the hull with adhesives or magnets. Small mines, like the one illustrated below, blast a hole in the bottom of the vessel. If placed under a magazine or a fuel bunker, they can be particularly devastating. Large mines can break the keel of a ship *(far right)*.

When a mine explodes underwater, it creates a high-pressure bubble of hot gas. Expanding, the gas sends out a strong shock wave at supersonic speed that hammers nearby objects. Within microseconds, water pressure quickly compresses the gas, which then expands again with a shock wave almost as strong as the first. This buffeting, which continues until the gas bubble reaches the surface, is the main reason that the relative effectiveness of an explosive is greater underwater than in air.

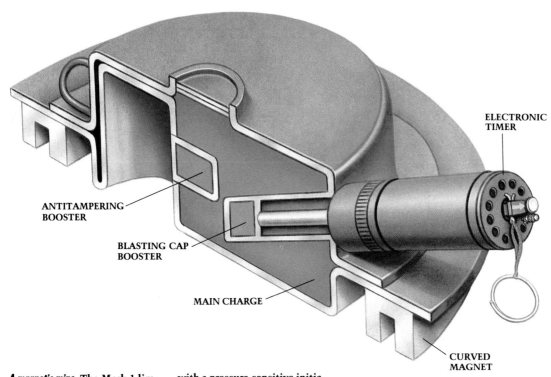

ANTITAMPERING BOOSTER

BLASTING CAP BOOSTER

MAIN CHARGE

ELECTRONIC TIMER

CURVED MAGNET

A magnetic mine. The Mark 1 limpet mine contains four pounds of HBX served by two boosters. One is activated by a blasting cap attached to an electronic timer, as shown here. Instead of the timer, the mine can be fitted with a pressure-sensitive initiator used chiefly against submarines. The other booster is for an antitampering device set into a well in the main charge. Six curved magnets hold the mine against a ship's hull.

Punching a hole. A Mark 1 limpet mine has sufficient power to punch a hole in the bottom of a ship weighing a hundred tons or more. Three or four such breaches can sink the vessels before the holes can be patched.

Breaking a ship's back. Larger mines, some with as much as 200 pounds of explosive, are hung below the keel. A huge bubble of gas from the explosion raises the ship at the center; the weight of the ends breaks the keel.

An Auspicious Comeback in Panama

4

Panamanian Defense Forces headquarters burn in Panama City after being strafed by U.S. Army and Air Force special-operations aircraft. They joined ground and sea commandos in spearheading Operation Just Cause, the 1989 invasion of Panama that toppled dictator Manuel Noriega.

Twenty minutes past midnight, December 20, 1989, and the United States stood on the brink of intervention in Panama. Major Kevin Higgins, commander of Company A, Third Battalion, Seventh Special Forces Group—the famed Green Berets—had been assigned a critical role. But as he waited with his troops for helicopters to land at Albrook Air Force Base—an American facility in Panama City—and carry them into action, Higgins could be pardoned if he felt a bit apprehensive about his mission.

Twice in as many days, his orders had been changed, each alteration adding responsibility and complexity to the task. At first, he had been told to send a three-man surveillance and reconnaissance team—plus an Air Force special-operations combat controller, who could call on an AC-130 Spectre gunship that would be orbiting nearby in case the commandos ran into trouble—to the Pacora River bridge along the Pan American highway, less than ten miles east of the Torrijos-Tocumen airfield complex. It consisted of the Torrijos International Airport on one side and a military facility, Tocumen Military Air Field, on the other. Torrijos-Tocumen would be an early objective of U.S. troops, and the reconnaissance team was to note any movement across the Pacora by troops of the Panamanian Defense Forces.

But headquarters had abruptly scrapped the surveillance idea and

111

ordered Higgins to hold the bridge against any enemy that might try to cross. For this task, he added himself and eleven Green Berets to the original number. They armed themselves with M16s, machine guns, and two varieties of light antiarmor rockets. The expanded team would be inserted by a pair of MH-60 Pave Hawks, Black Hawk helicopters that were specifically equipped for nighttime special operations.

Then, just half an hour later, the plan had changed again. As Higgins conducted final inspections, his face and those of his men blotched with camouflage grease paint, he had been notified that he could have the use of a third helicopter—a standard UH-60 Black Hawk transport—and that he should round up more men. Higgins had hastily tapped another eight troopers from his company, briefing them as best he could on the run.

Now the UH-60 was starting engines next to him on the Albrook helipad as the two MH-60s, loaded with the team's weapons, angled in from their station at Howard Air Force Base on the other side of the Panama Canal. Suddenly, just as the Black Hawks were settling to earth, the distinctive crack of AK-47 rifle fire sounded through the night. About a hundred yards away, a group of Panamanians had opened fire through the airfield fence at the hangar next to the helipad. Higgins and his men, who were standing in an open concrete-lined culvert, hit the deck, while the station's security detail hammered back at the muzzle flashes that were winking just beyond the fence. And at this point, while hugging the ground waiting for the attackers to be silenced, Higgins learned of yet another change in plans.

Originally, H-hour for U.S. action throughout Panama had been slated for 1:00 a.m.; now the Third Battalion's intelligence officer informed Higgins that because of security leaks, Higgins's operation, among others, had been pushed forward by fifteen minutes—to 12:45 a.m. Worse, advised the intelligence officer, a convoy of Panamanian vehicles had been spotted already rolling toward the Pacora River bridge. Estimated time of arrival, the major's new H-hour. Higgins and his men must get there first, but they now had scarcely fifteen minutes to travel the prearranged route, a twenty-five-minute flight to the bridge.

Gunfire continued to crackle around the base as Higgins and his men piled into the Black Hawks. In the lead MH-60, Higgins learned from the pilot, Chief Warrant Officer John Estep, that the landing zone had been changed. The original choice, near the bridge on the far side of the Pacora, was too small for three helicopters; a larger one was identified on the near side of the river. This shift rendered obsolete much of the mission minutiae of who would occupy which positions at the objective. Higgins and company would have to improvise.

Then the major informed Estep of the new H-hour. The pilot told the Green Beret commander that his chances of beating the convoy to the bridge verged on nil. With something like 170 U.S. helicopters, most of them blacked out, crisscrossing Panamanian skies at that moment, all air traffic had been coordinated to the fraction of a minute. To deviate from the flight plan—and count on seeing other aircraft through night-vision goggles and similar gear built into the MH-60—was risky in the extreme, but Estep understood the necessity. He would attempt a shortcut.

As the helicopters took off, Grenada seemed to echo loudly in the patchwork of last-minute orders that launched the Pacora River mission, but Panama would not be another gloomy chapter in the history of U.S. special operations—neither at the bridge across the Pacora nor in the numerous other actions taken in conjunction with conventional troops charged with toppling the brutal dictator of a friendly country. This time, the campaign generally would be well conceived and meticulously choreographed. Special-operations forces—the Army's Rangers, Green Berets, Delta Force, its helicopter and psychological-warfare units; the Navy's SEALs; the Air Force's AC-130 and Pave Low special-operations helicopter units as well as combat controllers—all would be integrated into the master plan; command, control, communication, and intelligence would be far better coordinated in Panama than they had been on Grenada. Most important, the commandos of all services would for the most part be assigned jobs that were clearly suited to their skills and character.

Not every mission would come off perfectly. Mistakes would be made, signals missed, and in one instance, unnecessarily high casualties taken. Intelligence would be wanting or erroneous in a number of cases, resulting in confusion, frustration, and further danger. Moreover, Panama's autocratic General Manuel Antonio Noriega, a prime target of the invasion, would prove unexpectedly elusive, the chase after him at times taking a farcical turn. Yet special-operations forces would achieve every objective (save for seizing the

General Noriega defiantly displays a decree, issued December 14 by his rubber-stamp Assembly of People's Power, naming him Panamanian head of state. The event signaled an end to nearly two years of unsuccessful American attempts to pry the reins of power from the dictator by persuasion and economic pressure.

dictator at the outset) and contribute mightily both to the downfall of an American nemesis and to the restoration of democratic institutions to Panama.

For years, the United States had been at odds with the Panamanian strongman. In 1987, the American Congress cut off all arms shipments to Panama after an investigation turned up strong evidence that Noriega was trafficking with the Colombian drug lords. The general then turned to Cuba for arms, and matters went from bad to worse. In February 1988, two U.S. federal courts in Florida handed down indictments accusing the Panamanian leader of drug running. Noriega, whose power derived from his position as head of the country's 16,000-man military, of which perhaps 3,500 were well-trained, well-armed, hard-case loyalists, merely laughed at American juridical procedures. Then, showing his contempt for his own country's democratic institutions, the general dismissed his country's freely elected president, promised a new vote for May of 1989, and then nullified the results when he took a thrashing at the polls. In October, a revolt erupted in the Panamanian Defense Forces among a number of mid-level officers; these PDF captains and majors actually arrested Noriega, but loyal units rushed to his rescue, and the coup was ruthlessly put down.

By this time, the United States had begun to think seriously of ridding Panama of this tyrant. President George Bush ordered General Maxwell Thurman, head of the Panama-based U.S. Southern Command, and Lieutenant General Carl W. Stiner, commander of XVIII Airborne Corps at Fort Bragg, North Carolina, to redraft an old contingency plan for action in Panama. Meanwhile, Noriega goaded his powerful northern neighbor. On December 15, he loudly announced to his handpicked national assembly that a state of war existed between the United States and Panama. The next evening in Panama City, an off-duty U.S. Marine lieutenant was cold-bloodedly shot and killed by PDF soldiers. A U.S. Navy lieutenant and his wife who witnessed the murder were seized by the same troops, who brutally beat the officer and threatened his wife with sexual abuse.

Enough.

A day later, President Bush set Operation Just Cause in motion, with H-hour set for 1:00 a.m., December 20. His generals intended to apply such overwhelming force so swiftly and at so many locations simultaneously that Noriega and his followers would be removed without grave damage to Panama or danger to its inhabitants—among them 50,000 military dependents and other U.S. citizens largely involved with operating the Panama Canal. Such considerations "caused us to come up with twenty-seven targets that should be attacked at H-hour," said General Stiner. The enterprise ultimately would require 27,000 American troops. Of these, 13,000 would be soldiers already in Panama, and 14,000 others would be flown from the United States. As a student of the Grenada failures, Stiner made sure, as he put it, that everyone in this considerable force would be singing off "the same sheet of music." A booklet listed the radio frequencies assigned every unit on each network. To ensure cooperation between ground troops and air support, Stiner furthermore established an air operations center that included representatives from every military element in Panama to control the air space over the combat zone.

Critical to the entire plan was the role of special-operations forces. There would be 4,150 such troops on hand for Just Cause, and Stiner, having commanded the Joint Special Operations Command at Fort Bragg, understood their strengths and limitations.

A central objective of the invasion force would be the PDF headquarters at the heavily fortified Comandancia complex in downtown Panama City. Its capture would be the responsibility of the Seventh Infantry Division and various other units. To facilitate that action, however, the Comandancia had to be sealed off from reinforcement by Noriega troops outside the capital. American intelligence knew that the PDF's reputedly tough Second Rifle Company was based at the Torrijos-Tocumen airfield, along with units of the Panamanian Air Force. Further, the equally competent Sixth and Seventh Infantry Companies were known to be quartered at an auxiliary field and military base called Rio Hato, seventy-five miles southwest of Panama City. Finally, Battalion 2000, the most powerful outfit of all and the one largely responsible for Noriega's rescue in the October coup, garrisoned Fort Cimarron, only half an hour by truck from Torrijos-Tocumen and another twenty minutes or so from Panama City.

Thus, a battalion of the 75th Ranger Regiment, specialists in airfield assault, would parachute in to take Torrijos-Tocumen and secure it both as a drop zone for the 82d Airborne and as an airstrip

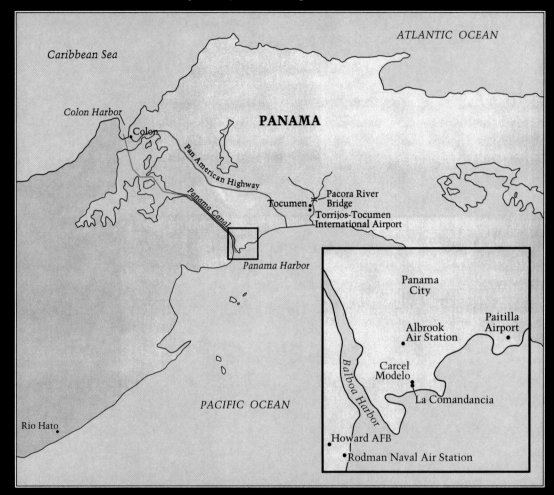

to land the Seventh Division. Another battalion from the 75th would descend on Rio Hato to liquidate that threat, while Special Forces Major Kevin Higgins and his Green Berets would stall Battalion 2000 on the east side of the Pacora River. Meantime, Delta Force and SEALs would be plying their trade by rescuing an imprisoned American citizen, preventing Manuel Noriega's escape, and hunting the dictator himself.

Despite every effort to disguise the invasion timetable, the news leaked out. On the evening of December 19, General Stiner learned of urgent warnings on PDF radio channels that "they're coming" and "the ball game starts at 0100 hours." The advance billing no doubt accounted for the convoy of Panamanian troops—almost certainly elements of Battalion 2000—racing toward the airport and

117

Panama City by way of the Pacora River bridge. Around midnight, Stiner advanced H-hour fifteen minutes, the maximum possible so late in the game. Though the change would not apply to the Rangers or other troops already en route from the States, he hoped to give his in-country forces, particularly the special-operations troops, at least a slight chance of surprise.

A Stitch in Time

It was almost exactly 12:45 when the three choppers carrying Major Higgins and his team whirled down over the Pacora River. With great skill, the pilot had led his three-ship fleet safely through all the traffic and had shaved ten minutes off the flight time. A heavy fog rose from the water, obscuring the forty-foot-tall bridge until the helicopters were almost upon it. As the aircraft overshot the mark, the Green Berets inside could count eight trucks in the approaching Panamanian convoy, now only 400 yards from the bridge.

Quickly reversing course, the choppers set the Americans down on the Panama City bank of the river. The troops leaped from the choppers with their weapons and scrambled up a steep embankment, overgrown with head-high elephant grass, to the highway leading across the 500-foot-long bridge. In the lead were two men from a ten-man team that, before H-hour had been advanced, was to have set up an ambush to block the bridge. Moving to the center of the road, one of the Green Berets launched a rocket. It dipped, hit the pavement, skidded under the truck, and exploded without setting the vehicle on fire. Nevertheless the convoy halted briefly, then slowly advanced—into a rocket fired by the second member of the ambush team to reach the road. Again no secondary explosion, but the convoy stopped again. By this time, the rest of the team had climbed the embankment. Machine-gun fire, more antitank rockets, and 40-mm grenades raked the trucks.

About this time, the combat controller shouted to Higgins that a Spectre, already orbiting overhead, was ready to assist. The major ordered his men to flatten themselves on the embankments and called for the Spectre. On the combat controller's order, the big AC-130 turboprop went to work. The aircraft commander opted for his rapid-fire 40-mm Bofors and 20-mm Vulcan cannons. Within minutes, three of the trucks had withdrawn, but the remainder had

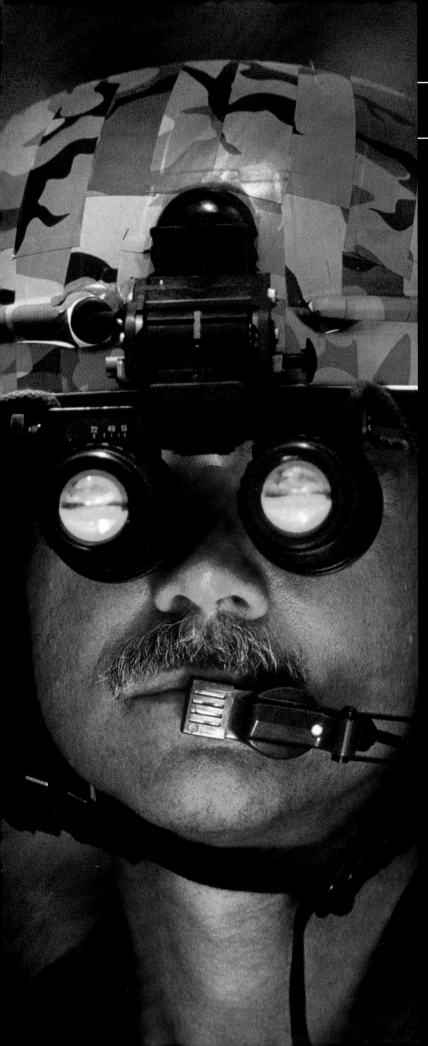

To See like an Owl

Darkness, the setting preferred for most special operations, can be as much an enemy as an ally. Though it may hide an attacker, it also obscures the objective. On the ground, it increases the risk of stumbling upon the enemy unexpectedly and of sending the engagement's crucial opening shots wild. For pilots, it makes nap-of-the-earth flying, the technique of skimming the ground that helps conceal approaching aircraft from the adversary, unacceptably hazardous.

Night-vision devices (NVDs) to help lift the veil of darkness date back to World War II. Early NVDs employed an infrared light to illuminate the target and an infrared-sensitive scope to view it. With an active system such as this, however, a similarly equipped enemy could easily spot the source of the infrared beam, turning the hunter into the hunted. This disadvantage spurred the development of passive NVDs, which emit no telltale signal of their own.

From the mid-1960s, passive night-vision gear has relied on a principle called image intensification to amplify minuscule quantities of ambient light. Since that technological breakthrough, designers have concentrated their efforts on making NVDs smaller, more sensitive, and more comfortable to wear. They are now de rigueur for almost all nighttime military undertakings and were widely used by American special-operations forces of all services in both Panama and the Persian Gulf.

A U.S. Air Force special-operations pilot peers through night-vision goggles. The gleam on the lenses comes from a coating that filters distracting reflections from the wind-screen.

How an NVD Brightens a Scene

Light itself cannot be amplified. Thus, to make a passive device that permits a soldier to see in the dark, some other approach to the problem had to be found. The solution was to convert light into electrons, the particles that whiz around the nuclei of atoms. Gallium arsenide releases electrons when struck by photons of light. Other compounds give off many such particles when struck by another electron, and chemicals called phosphors emit photons when bombarded by electrons. Assembled into an image intensification tube fitted with lenses on both ends, these elements can brighten a scene 3,000 times *(below)*.

First-generation passive night-vision devices relied solely on light at visible wavelengths, but the Generation 3 instruments make use of infrared light just beyond the visible spectrum. Even on the darkest night, when visible light is practically nonexistent, infrared energy is plentiful. Also, the reflective characteristics of different surfaces are more pronounced in the infrared band, thus creating an image that has greater contrast.

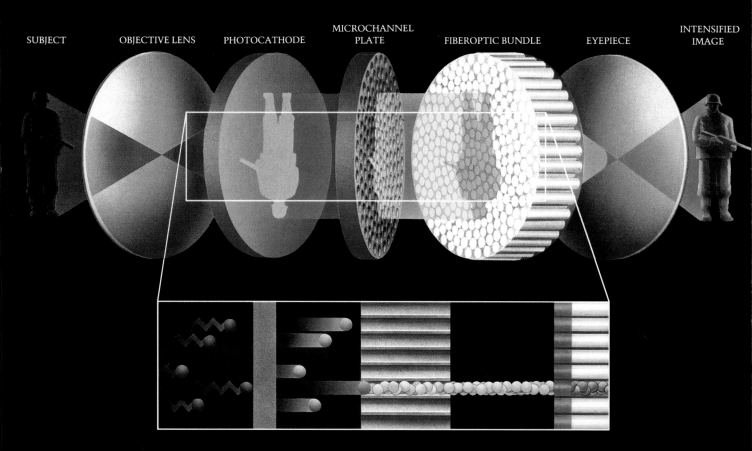

SUBJECT   OBJECTIVE LENS   PHOTOCATHODE   MICROCHANNEL PLATE   FIBEROPTIC BUNDLE   EYEPIECE   INTENSIFIED IMAGE

The illustrations above show the elements of a Generation 3 NVD and how they produce a bright image of a dim subject. Photons of light are focused by an objective lens on a photocathode coated with gallium arsenide, which discharges electrons when struck by photons *(bottom drawing)*. Voltage from the NVD's battery, raised from three to thousands of volts, accelerates the electrons toward the microchannel plate, a honeycomb comprising millions of microscopic glass tubes. Entering a tube, an electron dislodges hundreds of more energetic electrons from a coating inside, which strike a phosphor layer on a bundle of tiny optical fibers. The result is an upside-down image, turned right side up by an eyepiece.

The two photographs above, taken on an overcast, moonless night, show the dramatic effect of night-vision devices. On the left, the door of this rural outbuilding is almost invisible, as is the man crouching just outside the threshold. On the right, the same scene, photographed through an NVD, is a startling improvement. The door stands out in sharp contrast to the building's wall, and the shadowy figure of the man, rifle at the ready, is plainly visible.

NVDs can aid troops in distinguishing friend from foe at a distance. In the photo at left, an ill-defined figure can be discerned against the tree line at a distance of thirty yards. As the person moves closer *(center),* the shape becomes a man, who appears to be carrying something. At twenty yards *(right),* the man can be recognized as a soldier carrying an AK-47.

been damaged beyond salvation. Remarkably, none caught fire. Escaping PDF soldiers were slithering down the embankments, away from the highway. They, too, were taken under fire by the gunship. To discourage any survivors from fording the Pacora, Higgins ordered his men to lob an occasional grenade at the riverbank.

There was a flurry of excitement at 1:30 a.m., when the Spectre reported a column of automobiles speeding toward the bridge from the direction of Panama City. Tracers fired above the vehicles brought them to a halt. Spectre now radioed that there were three cars and that the occupants were dismounting. Higgins had his men send 500 rounds of machine-gun fire and thirteen grenades into the elephant grass along the highway. Concerned about the prospect of more enemy troops advancing from the rear, the major requested a second AC-130, and until dawn, one Spectre or another remained on station overhead. Around 2:00 a.m., a pair of Green Berets, placing a claymore mine on the road, spotted three armed soldiers advancing across the span. They shot and killed one man; the other two threw away their weapons and dived off the bridge. By 6:00 a.m., it was all over. Helicopters brought in a forty-five-man Green Beret quick-reaction team as reinforcements.

Despite an inauspicious start, Higgins and his exhausted team had achieved their objective without a single casualty. No aid for the Comandancia crossed the Pacora River bridge. In the bargain, a good part of Battalion 2000 had been dispersed, having lost four dead and seventeen taken prisoner.

Meanwhile, the Rangers of the 75th Regiment were focusing their attentions on the Panamanian Defense Forces at Torrijos-Tocumen and Rio Hato. Since early December, the 75th's three battalions had been practicing assaults at mock-ups of both installations in Florida; the men knew every detail of the objectives and had their timing down pat. The capture of Torrijos-Tocumen had to be almost chronographic in its precision; the commandos would have only forty-five minutes to parachute onto the twin airfields and secure Torrijos before the first paratroops of the 82d Airborne dropped from the skies.

The assault would be mounted by the First Battalion, plus Company C of the Third—731 Rangers in all, flying south in seven jet-powered C-141 Starlifters and four turboprop C-130 Hercules transports. While the formation was still some distance out, the first of two messages flashed to the commander in the lead aircraft, Lieutenant Colonel Tony Koren. It said that the invasion had been compromised. That did not come as a great surprise—a massive operation such as Just Cause could hardly pass unnoticed, especially when so much of the preparation had taken place within Panama—nor was the news particularly daunting. "From the past experiences the United States has been in, you know we're going to overwhelm them," said one Ranger. "We're so much better trained. Now it's like we're actually going to do something for real."

Message number two informed the commander of something more troubling. General Stiner had set H-hour for 1:00 a.m. partly because the last commercial flight scheduled into Torrijos-Tocumen, a Brazilian airliner, was to have landed before 11:00 p.m. Passengers would have had plenty of time to collect their luggage and depart. However, the Brazilian airliner had been delayed. It now sat on the ramp and empty, its passengers still inside the terminal. That complication would try the Rangers more severely than any resistance offered by the PDF.

Enemy air defenses were thought to consist primarily of two Soviet-built, Cuban-supplied ZPU-4s. These four-barrel, 14.5-mm heavy machine guns, which were capable of firing 600 rounds per minute, could be fatal to the transports loaded with Rangers. Machine-gun emplacements with smaller caliber weapons had been positioned around the Tocumen base. A hundred yards away from the Tocumen taxiway stood barracks that housed about 150 members of the Panamanian Air Force and 200 infantry troops of the PDF's Second Rifle Company.

Precisely at 1:00 a.m., an AC-130 Spectre demolished the gun positions suspected of containing the ZPU-4s—they turned out to be single-barrel .50-caliber machine guns—with its 105-mm howitzer. Seconds later, the gunship turned its weapons on the barracks, leveling them. At the same time, two AH-6 Little Bird helicopters flown by the Night Stalkers of the Army's 160th Special Operations Aviation Regiment (SOAR)—known as Task Force 160 six years earlier in Grenada—pounced on machine-gun positions with 7.62-mm machine guns and 2.75-inch rockets. The deadly little choppers next attacked the Tocumen control tower.

Firing ceased after two minutes and thirty seconds with the targets in ruins. Thirty seconds later, at 1:03 a.m., the transports arrived. They came in low, only 500 feet above the ground, streaming Rangers behind them. Off to one side of the transport formation, the AC-130 Spectre orbited like a guardian angel.

As the Rangers dangled in their parachute harnesses, they received only erratic fire. Some of it came from soldiers of the Second Rifle Company, who had started evacuating their barracks when they learned of the impending invasion. In the dark, none of the descending invaders was hit. About a dozen PDF soldiers defending the military terminal sprayed AK-47 and M16 rounds at Rangers shrugging off their parachute harnesses, wounding one man. A team of Rangers assembling after the jump encountered two PDF soldiers trying to escape in a truck. In the firefight that followed, Private First Class James William Markwell, a medic who had joined the Army nine months before in hopes of someday becoming a doctor, was shot and killed. He was the only American fatality during the assault on the airport complex.

American planners had figured that the Tocumen military airfield would be the tougher of the two targets, and the First Ranger Battalion concentrated there. In the event, however, Tocumen proved to be something of a cakewalk. Company A took the northern end of the airfield, seizing the Panamanian Air Force barracks and about a dozen helicopters and thirteen fixed-wing aircraft on the ramp. Bravo Company pushed south and established roadblocks at key arteries to secure the perimeter of the airfield where it bordered a swamp. Company C charged into the middle area, cleaning out the ruins of the Second Rifle Company barracks and rounding up the remaining PDF soldiers.

Time had been fleet. It was already after 2:00 a.m. with no sign of the 82d Airborne. Their drop zone along the Torrijos runway had long been secured, though firefights persisted on the fringes of the base. Then at 2:10 a.m., the sky overhead filled with the parachutes of the 82d's first wave. Alarmingly, however, they were hundreds of yards off the DZ and falling onto Tocumen among Rangers and sporadic firing. If the troops of the 82d mistook the Rangers for Panamanians, the potential for calamity, a "blue-on-blue" shootout, was very real. Fortunately, the quick-thinking Ranger commander, Lieutenant Colonel Bob Wagner, ordered a soldier with a bullhorn to shout up at the paratroops that they were dropping among friendlies—who then gave the unexpected visitors directions to their intended assembly area at the Torrijos civil airport.

Potent, Portable Firepower

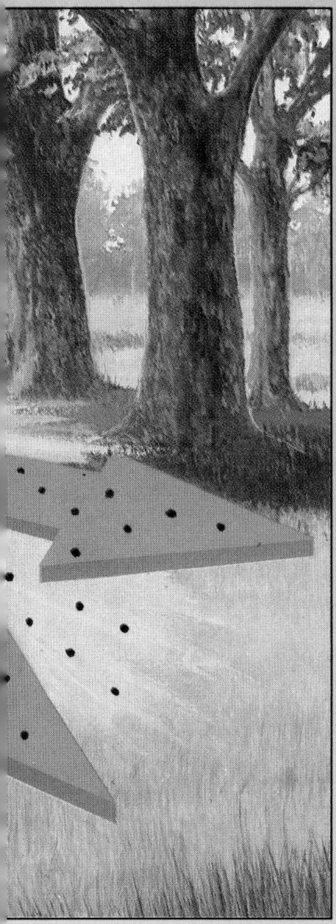

Equivalent to ninety men firing shotguns, the claymore mine is, pound for pound, one of the most destructive antipersonnel weapons in the special-operations arsenal. Popular among ground troops of all descriptions, it is a particular favorite with commandos. Often operating in small teams far from prompt assistance, they carry with them all the firepower they possibly can.

A versatile device, the claymore makes a potent opener for an ambush. Detonated afterward, it discourages pursuit by survivors. Commandos rig claymores with tripwires attached to initiators similar to the one shown on page 100 and set them out to cover the perimeter of an overnight campsite or leave them behind as booby traps.

Weighing only three and a half pounds, the claymore comes in a bag that can be slung across the chest bandoleer style. In addition to the mine itself, the bag contains an electric blasting cap, 100 feet of wire, and an M57 "clacker"—a small, hand-operated generator—to set off the mine. Also included is a test lamp for checking the circuit before a mission.

Though sometimes placed at chest height *(left)*, the claymore has pointed, folding legs for sticking into the ground. Aligning a simple sight with an object 150 feet away and eight feet above the ground ensures that the claymore fires neither too high nor too low. The blasting cap is screwed into one of the two wells provided for the purpose, then the mine is camouflaged and the wire laid to the firing position. After testing, the clacker, its handle secured by a safety wire, is hooked to the wire.

A sharp squeeze on the clacker produces an electric pulse, which detonates the claymore. In an instant, one and a half pounds of C-4 explosive sends 800 steel ball bearings, lethal out to 150 yards, speeding into the kill zone.

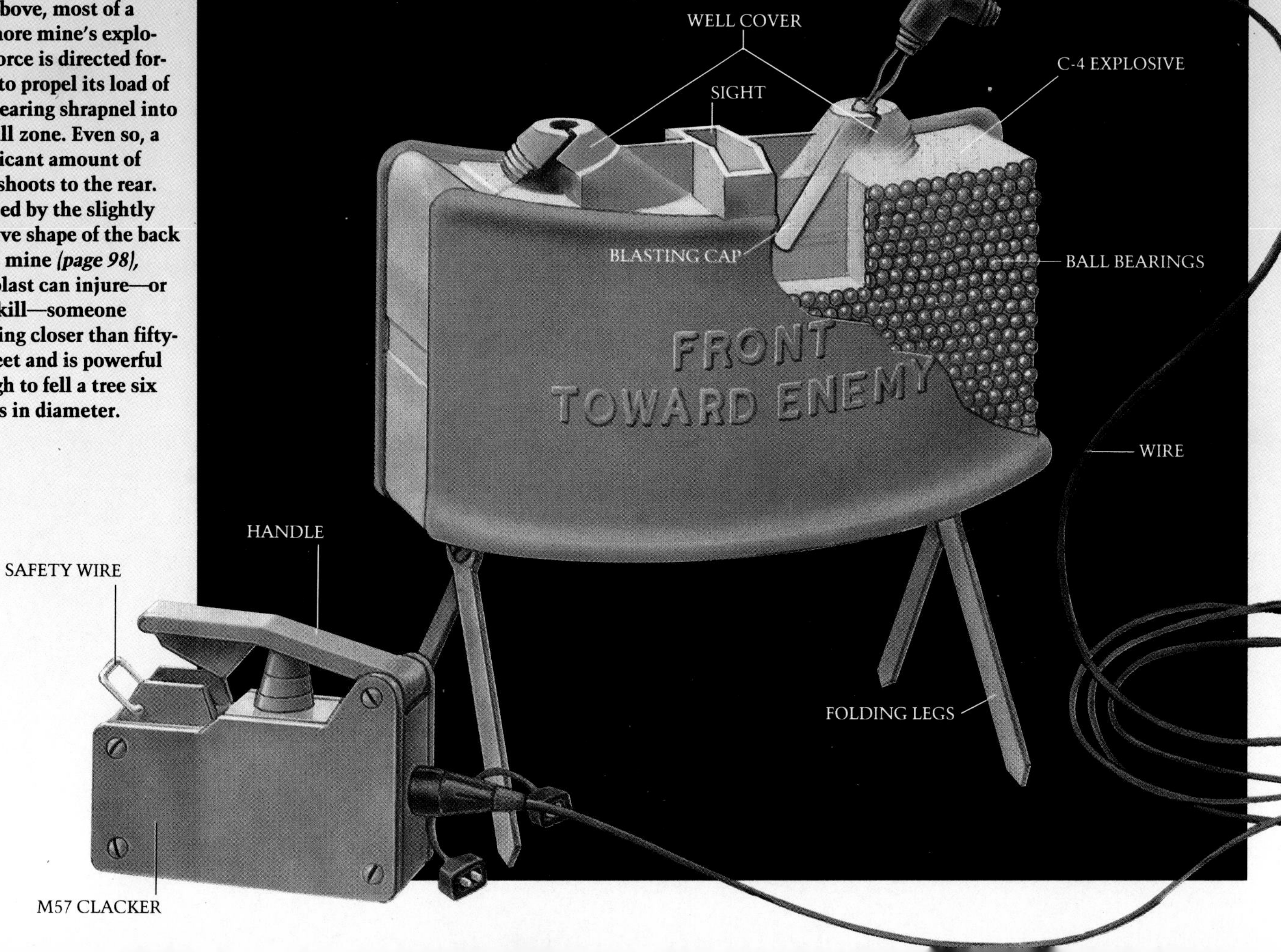

As shown in the illustration above, most of a claymore mine's explosive force is directed forward to propel its load of ball-bearing shrapnel into the kill zone. Even so, a significant amount of blast shoots to the rear. Focused by the slightly concave shape of the back of the mine *(page 98)*, backblast can injure—or even kill—someone standing closer than fifty-five feet and is powerful enough to fell a tree six inches in diameter.

WELL COVER

SIGHT

C-4 EXPLOSIVE

BLASTING CAP

BALL BEARINGS

FRONT TOWARD ENEMY

WIRE

HANDLE

SAFETY WIRE

FOLDING LEGS

M57 CLACKER

The job of securing Torrijos had fallen to the Third Battalion's Charlie Company under Captain Al Dochnal. His plan, which worked well at first, had been to use his three platoons to systematically clear outbuildings before dealing with the passenger terminal. Working their way toward the building, Dochnal's Second and Third Platoons had already taken nineteen airport workers into custody. More than a dozen of them had come from the fire station. As the Rangers had approached, a handful of firemen tried to make a run for it in a fire truck. When a stream of tracers crossed three feet in front of the speeding vehicle, however, it skidded to a stop, whipped around 180 degrees, and raced back to the station. Escape thwarted, the firefighters joined their mates as they heaped abuse on the Americans. One Ranger suggested lobbing a grenade as a "convincing device," but his squad leader demurred. Instead, he brought up a Spanish-speaking Ranger, who ordered the Panamanians to surrender with no further nonsense. In short order, fifteen firemen walked out of the station with their hands in the air.

Not far away, Charlie Company's Third Platoon ran into heavy fire as it approached the terminal. A squad led by a Sergeant Reeves scrambled up a maintenance stairway and into the building, where they spotted a pair of armed PDF soldiers scuttling into a men's room. Dashing after them with two of his mates named Eubanks and Kelly, Reeves yanked open the door and tossed in a grenade. Like many such facilities, however, this one had a foyer with interior doors that absorbed the blast and shrapnel. Unseen by the squad leader, whose view of the room was limited as he entered, one of the PDF had stood on the toilet in the first stall, and when Reeves entered the room, the Panamanian jabbed his AK-47 at the commando and let go three shots. Hot gases from the rifle muzzle scorched Reeves's face. Two bullets slammed into his right shoulder; the third smashed his collarbone.

Bleeding profusely but still conscious, Reeves thought as the Panamanian jumped on top of him as he fled: "At whatever cost, those two guys are gonna die. That was all there was to it." At that moment, Eubanks and Kelly crawled into the rest room to aid their leader. After pulling him into the hallway, they reentered the rest room, hurling grenades around a corner. Eubanks, who spoke a little Spanish, yelled for their adversaries to surrender but elicited only a torrent of obscenities. In response, the Rangers wounded one man in the neck, then shot the other in the head.

Five minutes had passed. Reeves would recover, and Eubanks was incredulous. "Those two idiots just holed themselves up in that latrine and thought they were going to take out a whole company of Rangers, and they were going to start with our squad," he said. "I guess they thought their cause was worth dying for."

By now, the First Platoon had eighty-eight Panamanians under guard after clearing a rental car facility and the bottom floor of the three-story terminal. Even so, knots of PDF soldiers were still at large in the building, shooting wildly as the Rangers spread out to secure it. Dashing up an escalator to the second floor, a squad from the Second Platoon took a burst of fire, then spotted five of the enemy running into the office of the Customs Police. Barricading themselves behind the heavy steel door at the entrance, the Panamanians started burning files. A Ranger rolled a grenade against the door. The explosion curled the bottom of the door up about a foot. Another grenade bowled under the door killed all five PDF men, but it also intensified the fire that, some speculate, may have been kindled to destroy evidence of drug dealing.

As smoke curled from the customs office, another Ranger squad was pounding along a third floor balcony when the men heard a woman crying hysterically and a male voice calling: "Don't shoot! Don't shoot! We're civilians." Looking over the balcony railing into a large darkened area below, the commandos saw hundreds of people milling about in terror—the passengers from the Brazilian airliner. The squad leader activated a blue chemical light and dropped it among the civilians, hollering for them to gather around it while his men hurried downstairs to escort them outside.

With the terminal burning, PDF troops still shooting, and too few Americans to clear the building systematically, Charlie Company was nervous. As they wrestled with such thoughts, a Panamanian civilian directed them to a baggage room on a lower level—and the ugliest situation of the night.

When two Rangers kicked open the door and leaped inside the darkened space, they saw with their night-vision goggles nine PDF soldiers, armed with AK-47 rifles, holding about twenty hostages at gunpoint. One was a wailing baby. The Rangers shouted at the Panamanians to drop their weapons. They refused. Stalemate.

Retreating through the doorway, the Americans repeated the call for the PDF soldiers to surrender. Each time, the Panamanians refused. A woman screamed: "Don't do anything! Just go away!

They're going to kill us if you try to do anything!" After a protracted standoff, during which the hostage takers fired at U.S. troops trying to outflank them, the situation was resolved, with the hostages walking unharmed from the room.

By 6:00 a.m., Torrijos International Airport was declared fully secured. No PDF troops would reinforce the Comandancia from this direction. In the aftermath of the fighting in the terminal, some of the Rangers stood guard over the nearly one hundred Panamanian airport workers while others fed and comforted almost 400 airline passengers. Remarkably, not a single civilian of any nationality had been killed or even injured. In their fruitless defiance of the Rangers at Torrijos-Tocumen, the Panamanians had lost thirteen killed and fifty-four captured. As for the Rangers, their busy night's work had cost one man killed, five wounded, and nineteen jump injuries. Some of the casualties, like the intrepid Sergeant Reeves, confessed that they were lucky to be alive.

The other half of the Rangers' Panama task force—the 75th's Second Battalion plus the two companies of the Third Battalion not assigned to seize Torrijos-Tocumen, 837 men in all—was charged with taking out the PDF at Rio Hato, a big base with three barracks areas, two motor pools, a communications center, a training facility, an ammunition depot, and a 10,000-foot airstrip. Rio Hato was garrisoned by the PDF Sixth and Seventh Infantry Companies. A combat engineering platoon brought the total to nearly 500 men armed with machine guns, mortars, recoilless rifles, and rocket-propelled grenades. In addition, they could muster nineteen American-made V-300 armored cars and three ZPU-4s. American intelligence analysts regarded the Seventh Company, who called themselves Machos del Monte (the Mountain Men), as well-trained, loyal to Noriega, and very likely to come to the aid of the Comandancia. The Machos, in General Stiner's view, were a "tough target." Noncombatants at Rio Hato complicated matters further. Within the compound where the troops lived stood a dispensary with a big red cross on the roof, and the training center was thought to house as many as 250 teenage noncommissioned-officer cadets. All in all, Rio Hato seemed to be a considerably dicier proposition than Torrijos-Tocumen.

Rehearsing the assault, the Rangers had duplicated the Rio Hato

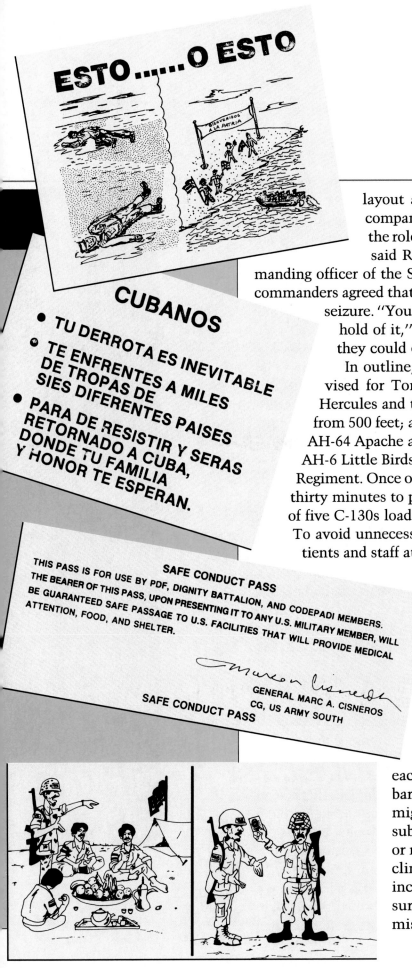

ESTO......O ESTO

CUBANOS

- TU DERROTA ES INEVITABLE
- TE ENFRENTES A MILES DE TROPAS DE SIES DIFERENTES PAISES
- PARA DE RESISTIR Y SERAS RETORNADO A CUBA, DONDE TU FAMILIA Y HONOR TE ESPERAN.

SAFE CONDUCT PASS

THIS PASS IS FOR USE BY PDF, DIGNITY BATTALION, AND CODEPADI MEMBERS. THE BEARER OF THIS PASS, UPON PRESENTING IT TO ANY U.S. MILITARY MEMBER, WILL BE GUARANTEED SAFE PASSAGE TO U.S. FACILITIES THAT WILL PROVIDE MEDICAL ATTENTION, FOOD, AND SHELTER.

GENERAL MARC A. CISNEROS
CG, US ARMY SOUTH

SAFE CONDUCT PASS

layout at Hurlburt Air Force Base, Florida. Two companies of the 101st Airborne Division played the role of the enemy, and "they gave no quarter," said Ranger Lieutenant Colonel Al Hunt, commanding officer of the Second Battalion. After three days of drill, commanders agreed that they had seen no finer example of airfield seizure. "You knew the soldiers were really going to grab hold of it," said one Ranger officer. "The boys knew they could do it."

In outline, the plan bore similarities to the one devised for Torrijos-Tocumen: Eleven C-130 turboprop Hercules and two C-141 jet Starlifters; a parachute drop from 500 feet; air support by a pair of AC-130s, two Army AH-64 Apache attack helicopters, and an equal number of AH-6 Little Birds of the 160th Special Operations Aviation Regiment. Once on the ground, the Rangers gave themselves thirty minutes to prepare the airstrip for a follow-on landing of five C-130s loaded with their vehicles and ammunition.

To avoid unnecessary injuries to the young cadets or to patients and staff at the clinic, planners searched for a way to neutralize the PDF infantrymen without blanketing the place with firepower. "We needed some system that would act to stun them without having to bomb the barracks directly," said General Stiner, and the Air Force came up with a suggestion—to employ the new F-117A stealth fighter-bomber armed with 2,000-pound laser-guided bombs. The Air Force gave Stiner a 95 percent assurance that a pair of F-117 pilots could each deposit such a bomb 100 yards from the barracks—close enough, they hoped, for the mighty explosions to shock the troops into submission without destroying the buildings or risking damage to the cadet quarters or the clinic. Stiner issued the go-ahead, though, to increase the chance that the barracks would survive, commanders later raised the near-miss distance to about 200 yards.

129

Precisely at 1:00 a.m., three minutes before the Rangers were scheduled to drop, two of the jet black F-117s roared over Rio Hato at 4,000 feet and released their ordnance. There is some dispute about what happened next. Early reports said that the lead pilot dropped his 2,000-pounder 300 yards from the barracks—and that his wingman was even wider of the target. "Our mission is to hit targets, not to miss targets," explained the flight leader, Major Greg Feest. "You train for years to hit things, and when you're told to go miss them, it's a different story." In essence, the absence of a well-marked aiming point on the field near the barracks meant that success relied more on the pilot's ability to accurately judge distance on the ground than on the F-117's capacity to score bull's-eyes. "We were told to hit a field, and that is precisely what we did," said one of the fliers.

At any rate, the effect disappointed everyone. Like other PDF units, the Sixth and Seventh Companies had been forewarned of the attack, and while a number of the troops stumbled dazedly from the barracks, many others were manning their weapons. Not that it did them much good. For as the thunder of the second huge bomb died away, the supporting Spectres, Apaches, and Little Birds started working over preassigned targets. One object was to smoke out the dangerous ZPU-4s. When one of the four-barrel machine guns opened fire, an Apache swept in and silenced it—or so it seemed. Moments later it began to shoot again. This time, as one Ranger related, a Spectre "put a 105-mm round in his watch pocket, and that was the end of that guy."

After ninety seconds, the Spectres and helicopters drew off to let the Rangers land. Not all the groundfire had been suppressed, and eleven of the thirteen transports took hits. Rangers inside remembered the bullets making a strange sort of ticking sound as they punctured the planes' aluminum skins. With the exception of one man wounded preparing to jump, no one was hurt until the troops started jolting onto the ground. Despite a diligent intelligence effort, the Rangers were unprepared for the terrain—broken ground punctuated by patches of jungle trees. Utility poles with street lights ran down the center of the complex. "A sporting drop zone," reflected the 75th's Commander, Colonel William Kernan.

The colonel personally doused the lights when his parachute got hung up in a power line, shorting out Rio Hato's electricity. Dangling from the shrouds, his toes six inches from the ground, Kernan

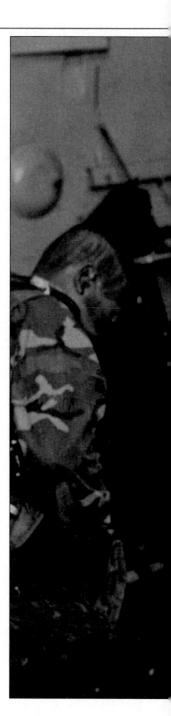

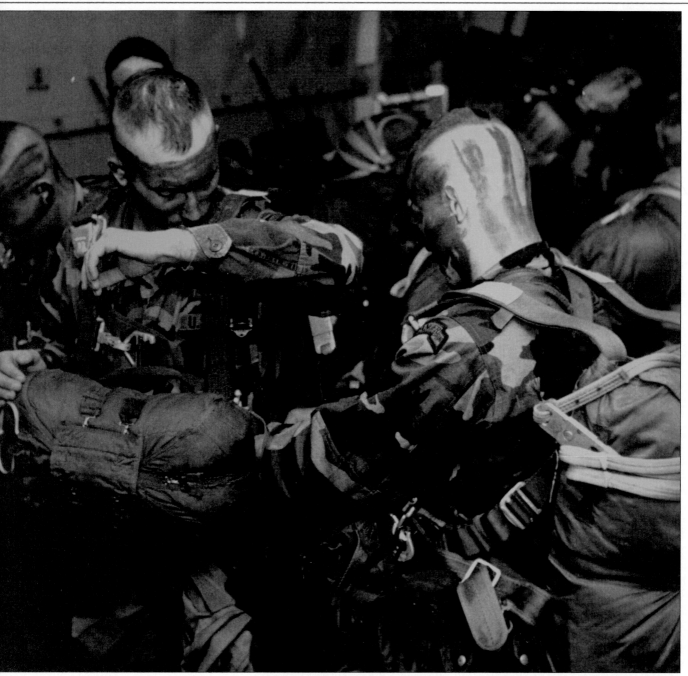

Rangers wearing jungle gear and camouflage check each other's equipment in
preparation for an airborne assault on the
air base at Rio Hato. American Ranger
paratroopers use a circular parachute

called the T-1 Para-commando for such
operations. It has a faster rate of descent
than more steerable, parafoil-style chutes,
shortening the window of vulnerability to
enemy groundfire.

slipped out of his harness just as the chute burst into flames. "Lightest landing at Rio Hato," he quipped later. Three dozen men—four percent—suffered jump injuries, fewer than anticipated.

In addition, there were Panamanians to deal with. One Ranger landed in a tree and came to a stop just a few feet above a PDF bunker where a soldier blasted away at other commandos. Hearing a rustle of leaves above him, the man looked up and fired a burst. Somehow it missed, and the paratrooper ended the encounter with a grenade. Another Ranger escaped death not once but twice. First, his chute failed to open properly, but it miraculously caught in the branches of a tall tree. Then, after he cut himself down and started toward the airstrip, three PDF troops bushwhacked him, shooting him twice in the chest. Thinking him mortally wounded, they left behind a black bandanna reading "Machos del Monte." Though grievously wounded, the sergeant would survive.

Confusion reigned. "It was a 360-degree firefight," said Colonel Kernan. In the barracks area, the combat proceeded from building to building, room to room. Retreating out the back of the buildings, the PDF would hide in nearby gullies and washes to waylay pursuing Rangers.

Concealed in falsely labeled crates, Soviet-made AK-47 assault rifles, possibly supplied by Cuba, were among the huge cache of weapons—machine guns, mortars, antitank rockets, and armored cars—that were uncovered by U.S. Rangers at the Rio Hato army base.

At least one commando died in this way. Yet the men fought with remarkable presence of mind. In the midst of the fighting, a Ranger burst into a building and for some reason—instinct, perhaps—held off hurling a grenade or spraying the premises with his M16. Inside huddled 167 frightened cadets.

Kernan called in the C-130s at 2:53 a.m. "The field was ready for air-land operations a lot sooner than that," he said. "But there were some minor skirmishes still going on, and rather than risk any of those aircraft, we made a decision to hold. We didn't need any of those supplies right away." Indeed, the transports were shot at as the pilots, wearing night-vision goggles, landed on the dark airstrip.

In taking Rio Hato, the Rangers killed thirty-four PDF soldiers and took another 362 Panamanian soldiers prisoner. Their own losses were four dead (two of them accidentally to fire from a Spectre gunship) and twenty-seven wounded; the score might have been worse had all the Machos been at home. Some of the troops, intelligence data later indicated, had been transferred to the Comandancia a few days earlier; others had melted into the jungle as the Rangers approached Panama. Once again no enemy reaction force made it into Panama City to relieve the Comandancia.

The fight for PDF headquarters saw commandos mainly in a supporting role. Capture of the fortress in downtown Panama fell to the men of the infantry and a Sheridan tank unit from the 82d Airborne. Yet the special-operations forces had a considerable hand in reducing the citadel's most formidable defenses.

Consisting of fifteen buildings surrounded by ten-foot-high cinder-block walls, some topped with grillwork, the headquarters compound filled an area about the size of two city blocks. The Comandancia proper, with walls of reinforced concrete two feet thick, stood three stories tall. Hundreds of Noriega's most loyal troops were garrisoned inside, supplied by an armory well stocked with guns and ammunition. Overlooking the compound on one side stood a sixteen-story high-rise, housing for members of Noriega's grandly named Dignity Battalion, a paramilitary collection of toughs and other misfits more aptly dubbed Dingbats by the Americans in Panama. Scores of these armed ruffians and many PDF soldiers lived in the building.

At 12:50 a.m. on December 20, two AH-6 Little Birds manned by SOAR pilots buzzed in just above the city skyline. Captain George Kunkel and Chief Warrant Officer Fred Horsley flew the lead helicopter. They made one pass with their 7.62-mm machine gun to clear snipers from the roof of the high-rise, then swung for a second run, this one against the Comandancia with 2.75-inch rockets.

From the apartment house balconies and windows, the Dingbats and PDF men let loose with a torrent of small-arms fire. Bullets missed the pilots but mortally wounded their helicopter. It lost

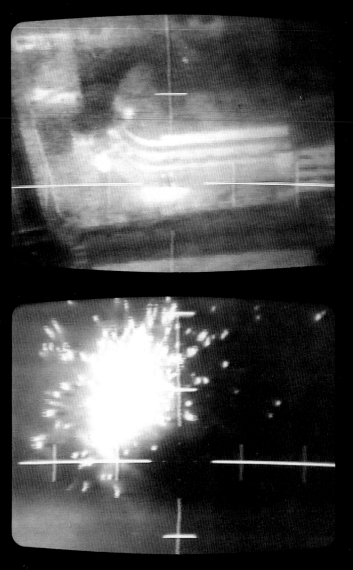

A single round, fired from the 105-mm howitzer mounted in an AC-130 gunship, demolishes the facade of a building in the Comandancia, headquarters complex for the Panamanian Defense Forces. The two pictures at left, taken through the aircraft's infrared viewing system, show the target and, seconds later, the explosion as the shell strikes. A photograph taken later documents the damage. AC-130s fired on trucks and other targets in Panama with the howitzer as well as their 40-mm cannons but avoided using their twin six-barrel Vulcans. Because they have a tendency to ricochet, the 20-mm bullets from these guns could have injured bystanders.

altitude rapidly and landed hard. Trailing smoke and flames, it skidded into a courtyard within the compound.

Amazingly, neither pilot sustained injuries in the crash. Kunkel and Horsley scrambled from their machine and took cover while Air Force AC-130s and Army Apache helicopters pounded the Comandancia defenses until dawn. Orbiting at 5,000 feet, a Spectre started in with its 105-mm howitzer. The SOAR pilots heard the thirty-two-pound explosive rounds slam into the PDF headquarters building, blowing off the roof and setting the third floor ablaze.

Panamanian soldiers occupying the upper floors of buildings inside the compound had been shooting over the wall, sniping at U.S. units assembled for an assault. But as the Spectres methodically chewed up the area, the snipers began shedding their uniforms and slipping out of the complex to disappear in the maze of streets or to take up new positions in the high-rise. Some two and a half hours after crashing, Kunkel and Horsley took advantage of a lull in the firing to scale the wall and join the American troops outside, taking with them a Panamanian who earnestly desired to surrender.

Next afternoon, General Stiner had one last job for the Rangers. Reports persisted of perhaps thirty PDF holdouts in the Comandancia compound and possibly another thirty inside Modelo Prison a block away. He wanted an outfit "proficient in clearing a building of that complexity," as he put it. That meant the Rangers, specifically Third Battalion's Charlie Company—the men who had performed so splendidly at Torrijos International Airport.

Captain Dochnal and his men were on their way to Howard Air Force Base for a rest when the call came in. It worried them. They had no plan, and Dochnal feared that the company, weary after the night's events, might take heavy casualties in the warren of cells, rooms, and hallways. After landing, Dochnal led his men at a run toward the Comandancia, making up a plan as he went.

At the prison, Dochnal's First Platoon attacked head-on with a combat assault aimed at the front door, the men covering each other and hurling grenades inside before entering. Amid the noise and smoke, one Ranger thought he saw a PDF man run up the stairs; several Americans pounded after him without success. All the cells, all the hallways were empty save for some corpses that had resulted from earlier action at the prison. Dochnal left a squad on the prison roof; they would serve as an observation and sniper position while his Second and Third Platoons dealt with the Comandancia.

First, the Rangers blew their way into a small gymnasium opposite the Comandancia, ready to fire 40-mm grenades into the compound if necessary while one man raced across the street and blew open a gate with a satchel charge. Once inside, he bowled a grenade that shattered glass doors to the main building. Before the smoke cleared, the two platoons swarmed into the building, then split up, some going right, others left, and the rest straight to the rear.

On the ground floor and in the cellar, no PDF had remained to fight. Methodically, the squads cleared out the upper stories, room by room. Again, no one. Rifles leaned against the wall at the back door testified to the flight of the PDF. Dochnal noted that for all the aerial pounding by AC-130s, parts of the building's interior remained surprisingly intact. "The PDF could have had a company in there," he said, "and they would not have been hurt."

A Rescue in 360 Seconds

Kurt Frederick Muse, like many other American civilians in Panama, woke with a start as Operation Just Cause jumped off. This gringo was unusual, however, in that his bed stood in a cell at Modelo Prison. Muse had been arrested by Noriega's henchmen the previous April. In the past few weeks, as tensions escalated between the United States and Panama, Muse had been assigned a special guard, who told the American that he had been ordered to execute him immediately in the event of hostilities. Muse had asked: "Will you really kill me?" "Yes," replied the guard unhesitatingly.

Muse, a longtime resident of Panama and a member of the Rotary Club, languished in prison because he had helped organize a group of fellow Rotarians, all Panamanians, to foster opposition to Noriega. He and his friends started by acquiring a few forbidden police radio scanners and monitoring PDF communications. "I overheard drug deals being transacted over the air in a relaxed and routine manner," said Muse. "I remember a conversation between two Noriega cronies about a major drug transfer planned for the parking lot of a popular supermarket. As a token of good will, the client wished to donate fifteen M16 rifles to Noriega."

Offered powerful radio transmitters and even television equipment by another Panamanian opposition group, the band of patriots began broadcasting three times daily, calling themselves Radio Libertad. Enraged, Noriega sent direction-finding teams to track them down, but they eluded capture by frequently moving their transmitting gear. Eventually, however, the secret police caught up with Muse through an informant. Then came sixty hours of relentless questioning and accusations of being a CIA agent. Muse denied that charge but eventually confessed: "I'm Radio Libertad."

There followed a nightmare of imprisonment. Though Muse himself suffered little physical abuse, he witnessed the travails of other prisoners. "The sound of a man being tortured," said Muse, "is indescribable." By applying the most severe pressure, the U.S. embassy won concessions for Muse—food deliveries and visits from American officials, including an Air Force doctor. At meetings in the prison infirmary, Muse told the doctor about his menacing new trusty and informed him whenever he changed cells.

That turned out to be a smart thing to do, because someone in the American government decided that Muse would be rescued. Perhaps the impetus came from learning that the impending invasion would probably trigger an American's execution. Maybe Muse really was a CIA agent, a status that called for a special effort to save him. Whatever the motivation, Delta Force got the call.

Muse recalls being jolted awake shortly before 1:00 a.m. on December 20 by a long burst of machine-gun fire outside. Then came return shots, shouts, and running footsteps. He next heard a great crash as a 105-mm round from an AC-130 Spectre gunship blew a hole in the Comandancia. All the lights in the prison went out.

Then an explosion boomed inside the prison, followed by a second and a third, coming closer. A submachine gun burped nearby, then Muse saw light beams stabbing through a haze of smoke that had rolled into the corridor. Suddenly, a figure materialized before his cell. "The guy looks like Darth Vader," remembered Muse. "He's wearing a funny-looking helmet, funny-looking uniform, and has a funny-looking weapon."

The apparition was a Delta Force commando, dressed all in black—bullet-resistant helmet, fire-retardant jumpsuit, flak jacket—and carrying a 9-mm submachine gun mounting a flashlight.

"Muse! You okay?" shouted the Delta trooper. In the excitement, the name sounded like "Moose."

"Yo!" replied the prisoner.

Details of a Prison Break

The well-synchronized rescue of American Kurt Muse began at H-hour, when a Little Bird helicopter landed Delta Force troops atop Modelo Prison *(1)* to snatch their quarry from his cell on the second floor *(2)*. Some of the commandos blew open the rooftop door *(3)* for others to enter and extricate Muse and hustle him into the chopper. After rising thirty feet, it was hit by gunfire. Fortunately, the pilot was able to keep from crashing into the street next to the prison *(4)*. He then scooted along to the nearest intersection, where he turned left *(5)*. Reaching a courtyard *(6)*, he climbed to a height of about three stories, when the helicopter was struck again. This time it went down for good, bouncing against a building before hitting the street. All of this action took place within sight of the Comandancia *(7)*.

The morning after the invasion, a Panamanian newspaper published this photograph of the Little Bird helicopter used the night before to pluck anti-Noriega activist Kurt Muse from Modelo Prison. A photographer from *La Republica* took the shot, which clearly shows side benches added to provide extra seats for Muse's Delta Force rescuers, minutes before a U.S. armored personnel carrier arrived to drag the chopper away.

"Stay down!" the operator ordered. "I'm going to blow the door!"

Flat on the floor, Muse sensed a flash through his tightly closed eyelids, heard a boom, and then the commando was inside, saying, "We're here to take you out! We're going to the roof! We've got a chopper! You're going to get in the middle! Do you understand?"

Muse said he did. His rescuer helped him into a flak jacket and clapped a helmet on his head. Three other commandos joined them as they raced up two flights of stairs to the roof, past five dead guards and a handcuffed live one. Outside, another four Delta Force operators crouched facing away from one of the Little Bird helicopters flown by the 160th SOAR. Muse could see rotors whirling and benches along the fuselage for additional seating.

Muse's saviors bundled him into the rear of the cabin, with a commando left and right. As the other six Delta Force troopers strapped themselves onto the exterior benches, three to a side, the SOAR pilot fed in power and the Little Bird lifted off the roof. From landing on the roof to takeoff, the whole operation had taken less than six minutes.

But then, just as the helicopter cleared the building, heavy groundfire caused the machine to lurch violently and fall off toward the ground from a height of about seventy feet. By some miracle of flying, the pilot managed to avoid smacking the ground and rotored along a street in front of the prison. Landing skids grazing the pavement, the pilot steered around a corner into a courtyard, then lifted the chopper to a height of thirty feet or so.

Bullets zipped all around, whanging into the helicopter. Finally, the pilot could hold it aloft no longer. With a screech of metal, the Little Bird hit hard, left skid first, and slid to a halt. Muse was merely stunned, but the three troops strapped onto the left bench were seriously injured. Another man had taken a round in his chest. The tip of the chopper's rotor clipped the helmet of a rescuer helping Muse from the aircraft, lacerating his scalp and briefly knocking him unconscious. Muse looked into the bloody face, and the eyes popped open. "Hey, Moose! You okay?" asked the commando.

Dragging their casualties with them, the commandos hastily set up a defensive position next to a parked Jeep Wagoneer. One of them clicked on an infrared strobe light and held it up. Orbiting overhead for just such a contingency, the pilots of a SOAR MH-60 Pave Hawk

140

ⓁⓐⓇⓔⓟⓤ́ⓑⓛⓘⓒⓐ

AÑO XII   B/.0.20

PANAMA, R. DE P., MIERCOLES 20 DE DICIEMBRE DE 1989

...ia heroi- / ejército

genocida norteamericano en momentos que violaba el espacio aéreo panameño, durante la invasión armada contra el pacífico pueblo panameño. Esto demuestra con evidencias palpables que los genocidas de Bush no son invencibles, que también mueren y podemos derrotarlos, como lo hace el heroismo de nuestro valiente pueblo. El helicóptero cayó en un patio de la Huerta Sandoval en El Chorrillo. (Foto de Rogelio Achurra)

saw the strobe with their night-vision goggles and radioed for help. Moments later, a column of armored personnel carriers came roaring down the street to complete the rescue. They transported Muse to an assembly area; then he flew by Black Hawk to Howard Air Force Base, where a doctor examined him. Upon asking if he could see the men who had saved him, Muse was taken to a field hospital where three of the injured lay on stretchers. "These guys were beat to hell," Muse recalled. "Blankets over them. IVs, stitches, clotted blood, casts. They really looked bad, but they were all smiling."

Muse knelt beside them. "You guys saved my life and I'm eternally, eternally grateful," he said. Later he remembered that "I felt like hugging these guys. Kissing them. I couldn't speak."

A Delta Force colonel standing nearby told him: "I want to thank you for talking to my troops. My guys train for a lot of missions, and they never get to do many of them. But for this one they trained long and they trained hard and they got to do it."

Dictator on the Lam

Shortly after parachuting onto the Torrijos-Tocumen airport, a Ranger fire team set up a blocking position astride an access road to the military side of the field. Abruptly, a small automobile whipped around a curve and raced toward the Tocumen airstrip. The commandos opened fire. Screeching to a halt, the vehicle doused its headlights, raised a cloud of dust from the dirt road as it spun around, and accelerated out of view.

Unbeknown to the Rangers, one of the people in the car was Manuel Antonio Noriega, attired in red underwear. He had been spending the night with a prostitute at Tocumen's Ceremi Recreation Center, a one-time motel transformed into a brothel and officer hangout for the PDF's Second Infantry Company. Noriega's nocturnal activities had been interrupted by the booming howitzer of an AC-130 Spectre gunship softening up Tocumen's defenses for the Ranger assault.

Without bothering to dress, Noriega had dashed out of the rec center hoping to escape in a Panamanian Air Force plane. Not until an hour later, when other Rangers searching the recreation center found Noriega's shoes and his gaudy general's uniform with nametag attached, did anyone realize how close the commandos had come to apprehending the tyrant at the outset.

To the United States, the capture of Noriega and his arraignment as a drug dealer and a common criminal was a goal every bit as important as dismantling the dictator's repressive regime. "Go for the head of the snake," said General Stiner. Regarding the task as tailor-made for special-operations units, he assigned it to Delta Force and the SEALs.

Under a complex plan, commandos were to choke off every avenue of escape for Noriega and, having tracked his movements beforehand, capture the man himself. As it turned out, the most carefully laid stratagems would come unraveled in the confusion of combat, resulting in tragic casualties for one of the military's finest units. The dictator himself would prove to be slippery as an eel. A frustrating game of hide-and-seek would occupy the better part of four days, with the fugitive always a half step ahead of his pursuers. Yet in the end, the special-operations forces would accept Noriega's surrender and see him packed off to a jail cell in Miami.

A Navigator You Can Hold in One Hand

Knowing your location is vital in combat, especially for special-operations troops. Missing an extraction rendezvous by a hilltop or two, for example, could easily leave them stranded—or worse. Yet matching a position on the ground with a spot on a map has always been trying. Errors are especially likely at night or in terrain with few distinctive features.

A remedy has come in the form of the Global Positioning System (GPS), an array of navigation satellites *(overleaf)* that tells troops their location, day or night, through a hand-held receiver *(below)*. During the 1991 Persian Gulf War, American commandos ranging far into Iraq used GPS not only to find their way, but to pinpoint Iraqi missile sites for air attack—among other feats.

Special-ops commandos, of course, had no monopoly on this gear. Thousands of receivers were shipped to the Kuwaiti theater of operations, enough to equip virtually every platoon and many aircraft with this means of finding their way.

After a GPS receiver is turned on and the side-mounted antenna rotated skyward, pressing the POS button starts a position-finding process inside the unit. Within three and a half minutes, the receiver displays its location, then updates the reading every second. The unit has other helpful features. WPT allows the entry of coordinates for way points, checkpoints en route to a destination. ROUTE allows the storage of several way point sets. NAV shows bearing and distance to a destination from any point along the way, while VEL calculates average speed since setting out. TARGET, followed by the distance (acquired by laser range finder) and bearing to an objective, displays its coordinates, handy for calling in artillery or air strikes. SETUP is used to orient the unit when it is new.

A Common Point on Three Spheres

Simultaneously elegant in its simplicity and mind-boggling in its complexity, GPS relies on a basic fact of geometry: A point a given distance from a satellite overhead must lie somewhere on the surface of a sphere—or a circle on the earth's surface. Additional satellites and circles reduce this initial infinity of positions to one. Accomplishing this feat requires accurate clocks and computers on board the satellites, as well as inside GPS receivers.

The computer aboard each satellite is programmed to generate a repeating string of ones and zeros. In it, the spacecraft continually identifies itself by number and describes its position in its orbit. An on-board atomic clock ensures that the code of ones and zeros is transmitted on a rigidly maintained schedule.

Transmitted to earth, codes from four satellites are picked up by a receiver. After identifying each spacecraft, the receiver matches its code to an identical one generated internally. By measuring the delay between its own production of a code segment and the arrival of an identical section from a satellite, the receiver can calculate the distance to the spacecraft, given that the signal travels at the speed of light. All four signals are needed to solve the complex set of equations that yields a position. However, the fundamental geometry of the situation is most clearly revealed in the three-satellite illustrations at right.

Control stations on the earth constantly monitor the satellites' signals and beam up adjustments to compensate for any clock errors or variations in orbit. The result is extraordinary precision. Troops equipped with GPS receivers can pinpoint their location to within sixteen meters.

A GPS receiver on the earth—aboard a ship, for example—calculates its distance from an orbiting Navstar satellite and determines that the vessel lies somewhere along the circle below, every point of which is the same distance from the spacecraft.

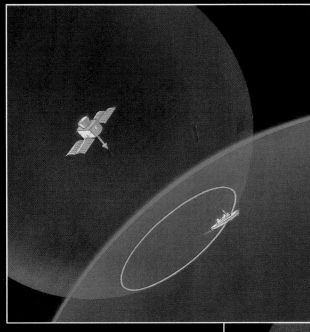

For simplicity, the illustrations above show how GPS functions for a receiver located at sea level. But as depicted at right, the position of an aircraft in flight or a soldier on a desert plateau is determined by the same method. There is no ambiguity because the spheres do not intersect when they are projected as white circles at sea level. Consequently, GPS receivers have an inherent ability to display height above sea level.

Next, the receiver figures the distance to a second satellite, yielding another circle *(red)*. Because the receiver must lie on both circles, its position has to be at one of the two points where the circles intersect.

The GPS unit then measures the distance to a third satellite. The resulting circle *(yellow)* intersects the first pair at one of the two points established by the second satellite, pinpointing the ship's location, which lies on all three circles.

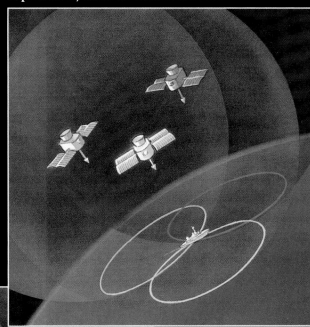

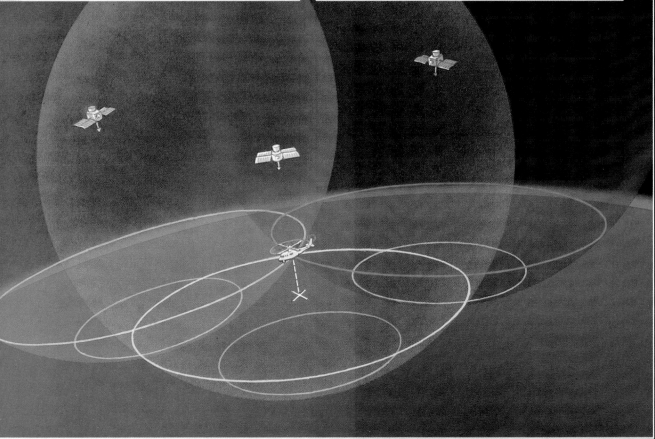

The essential task of shutting down escape routes fell to Navy special-operations troops. Three operations were planned. First, SEALs aboard two Navy river-patrol boats and two Army landing craft closed off the harbor at Colón on the Caribbean side of the isthmus. Warning all vessels attempting to exit the port that it was closed, they fired a shot across the bow of any ship, flying whatever flag, if the master seemed slow in turning back.

Second on the target list was a sixty-five-foot Panamanian patrol boat, the *President Porras,* in which Noriega might seek to escape. Tied up at a pier in Balboa harbor, the *President Porras* could also fire at low-flying helicopters and other aircraft transiting the area on their way to and from H-hour targets. At 11:30 p.m., H-hour minus one hour and fifteen minutes, four SEAL divers, wearing black wet suits and carrying two twenty-pound satchel charges containing C-4 explosive, motored out of Rodman Naval Air Station, then slipped into the water and swam toward the patrol boat. Undetected, the SEALs attached their explosives to the vessel's propeller shafts, then swam away. At precisely 1:00 a.m., a loud, gratifying boom sounded from the boat. So far, the SEALs were batting 1,000.

Panama City's Punta Paitilla Airport, a private facility with an airstrip that ended at the shore of Panama Bay, was the third target. Noriega kept a personal Learjet there. Planners might have ordered it destroyed in any number of ways—by naval gunfire or AC-130 strike, to name two. But doing so risked damage and civilian casualties, inasmuch as one of Panama City's wealthiest neighborhoods bordered the airfield on the north and west, and a score of light planes owned by prominent Panamanians dotted the field. To keep the operation as clean as possible, SEALs were to be sent in.

The job seemed simple enough. Noriega kept his Learjet in the middle hangar of three at the north end of the field. SEALs were to disable the plane by slashing its tires or jamming the landing gear, and to block the runway with other planes and vehicles. Intelligence about Punta Paitilla indicated that only a small maintenance crew would be on duty at H-hour. They and a handful of lightly armed civilian security guards—"rent-a-cops," one official had called them—seemed to offer the only complication. As they had the *President Porras* mission, commandos practiced the Paitilla assault before enplaning for Panama. Observers deemed the rehearsals to be solid successes, but in the event, the effort to wreck Noriega's plane would prove a costly one.

U.S. Army Special Forces troops frisk Panamanian soldiers found hiding in the bush. The Green Berets scoured the countryside after the fighting ended, rounding up stray Noriega supporters to forestall a guerrilla warfare campaign that could have jeopardized the nation's new democratic government.

146

Near midnight, a U.S. Navy patrol boat, idling about a mile off-shore in Panama harbor, launched fifteen Zodiac rubber boats holding three platoons of sixteen men plus an Air Force combat controller to communicate with an AC-130 gunship orbiting overhead in case the SEALs might need precision air support. A seven-man command-and-control unit headed by Commander Thomas Mc-Grath would remain offshore during the operation.

Led by Lieutenant Commander Patrick Toohey, the Zodiacs moved in close offshore and anchored near the dimly lighted seaward end of the runway. Swimmer scouts slipped over the side of one boat to reconnoiter the bay end of the airport. As Toohey awaited word from his advance men, he received news that H-hour had been moved up from 1:00 a.m. to 12:45. Already working to a tight schedule, he hurried his platoons ashore before the scouts reported. Going in blind was against doctrine and could have been disastrous; fortunately, the scouts found the beach deserted.

Rejoined by the reconnaissance squad, the three platoons of SEALs crept stealthily through an opening in the airport fence. As the men assembled in the grass edging the runway, Toohey received another disturbing radio report. A Panamanian helicopter had just taken off from Colón, thirty-five miles away; it might be heading for Paitilla with Noriega on board. This information—false, as it happened—moved Toohey to speed two platoons toward the hangars at a quicker than usual pace in order to intercept the helicopter. Though not running, the men were moving quickly and incautiously enough to be spotted halfway along the runway. Panamanian voices shouted at the SEALs in Spanish, telling them to get off the airfield; the Americans yelled back, ordering the Panamanians out of the area. Neither group did the other's bidding.

As the SEALs were moving into position to attack the hangars, one squad of eight men entered the glare of lights illuminating the tarmac. A number of PDF soldiers, presumably sent to guard the Learjet after word of the invasion leaked, had concealed themselves behind oil drums. Alerted by all the shouting, they raised their AK-47s and cut loose with a burst of automatic fire. The soldiers knew what they were doing; using a technique known as skipping, they kept their aim low, so that even the short rounds ricocheted off the pavement and added to the hail of lead cutting into shins, legs, and lower torsos. In an instant, seven of the nine SEALs were hit, one of them fatally. Then a firefight started between the PDF troops

Noriega's personal Learjet, once a potential means of escape for the dictator, stands crippled in a hangar at Punta Paitilla Airport after a SEAL blasted it with a high-explosive round from a 40-mm grenade launcher. Detonating on contact with the plane, the grenade blew a hole in it almost the size of a cabin window, just aft of the cockpit.

and a second squad of SEALs moving to assist the first. Overhead, the Spectre crewmen witnessed the slaughter on their low-light-level television cameras. They waited for the order to fire. The Air Force combat controller, who had remained with the third platoon near the south end of the runway, was trying desperately to make that call. But no matter which frequency he tried, he could not raise the gunship.

When shooting erupted, Toohey had started running toward the action with his radio operator shouting "H.E.! H.E.!," a call for his men to start blasting at their antagonists with high-explosive grenades and antitank rockets. They attacked with a fury. "We were filling that hangar with rounds; 40-mm grenades were going everywhere," one SEAL recalled. For almost a minute the storm of fire continued. Return fire from the Panamanians as they withdrew wounded additional SEALs and killed some of those wounded in the initial burst of fire. Altogether, the SEALs had four dead and eight wounded. A Panamanian intelligence officer later revealed that three PDF soldiers had died in the attack while eight injured were carried away by their comrades.

An hour and twenty minutes passed after the shooting stopped before Army medevac helicopters, held on the ground because of the heavy air traffic, arrived from Howard Air Force Base. At dawn, helicopters brought a fourth platoon of sixteen SEALs, and together with the three dozen still on their feet, they held the airfield until relieved by Rangers.

At the height of the action, one of the 40-mm grenades had blown a hole in the Learjet, disabling it. Thus, the SEALs had carried out their mission to the fullest, but at the cost of 25 percent casualties and numerous questions about the operation. Why the Spectre and the combat controller could not communicate remained a mystery. There was some talk, denied by the Air Force, that the radios on that particular aircraft malfunctioned at a critical time. Others suggested that the combat controller and the Spectre crew, both frantically switching channels, had simply missed each other. Some wondered how much help the Spectre would have been even in the absence of communications glitches, since the SEALs had taken most of their casualties during the first few seconds of shooting.

Other questions revolved around whether too small a force had been sent and whether SEALs, being most experienced at reconnaissance and covert operations, should have been involved in the first place. General Stiner and other commanders insisted that the assignment was appropriate. In the end, the official explanation—not an unreasonable one—laid the high casualties to the fortunes of war. Said one special-ops commander sadly: "Even well-trained units make tactical mistakes once in a while."

In sending SEALs to remove Noriega's means of escape, Stiner and others in charge of Just Cause had merely hoped to cover their bets that the dictator would be captured before he had an opportunity to flee. Indeed, the hunt for the Panamanian strongman had been under way for weeks before the actual invasion. As far back as the October coup attempt, U.S. intelligence and special-operations teams established an around-the-clock "Noriega Watch," monitoring the dictator's every move and communication. But it was a two-way game. As time went on, the wily Noriega became ever more elusive. He broadcast radio messages with false itineraries, sent out decoy convoys, shifted location as often as five times a night, and on December 19, the eve of invasion, he gave his trackers the slip altogether.

At 6:00 that evening, the Noriega watchers knew their quarry to be in Colón at the Atlantic end of the Canal. Shortly thereafter the surveillance picked up a motor-

Delta Force troopers, recognizable in part by their unusual headgear and their German-made submachine guns, patrol outside the Vatican Embassy in Panama City. Just Cause planners had overlooked the embassy as a possible sanctuary for Noriega, and the commandos took up these positions only after he was inside.

cade of trucks and buses leaving Colón headed south along the main artery to Panama City. Halfway there, the column pulled a favorite Noriega stunt. Part of the convoy turned off for Torrijos-Tocumen airport, while the rest continued toward Panama City and the Co-mandancia, where an honor-guard ceremony awaited the man who strode quickly from one of the vehicles. Was he Noriega? The watchers were skeptical, but in the meantime, the other vehicles entered the sprawling, well-guarded Tocumen military complex—where the stalkers could not follow. Noriega had vanished, not to be seen again during the twenty-four hours or so remaining before the invasion got under way.

Having no clear idea of the dictator's whereabouts at H-hour, SEALs and Delta Force operators raided no fewer than seven residences they knew Noriega to frequent. All in vain. The fugitive, in those moments, was escaping from the Rangers at Tocumen, and for the next four days, he led his pursuers on a merry chase around Panama. At one point, early in the chase, Noriega turned up at the government radio station, not yet secured by U.S. forces. "Our slogan is to win or die," he broadcast. "Not one step back." President Bush placed a million-dollar bounty on Noriega's head, prompting a number of his aides to offer opinions as to his possible whereabouts. Between December 20 and 24, Delta Force and SEALs mounted no fewer than forty operations trying to catch the man. On one raid, the pursuers burst into a Noriega hideout to find the coffee still warm; on another occasion, Noriega fled so hastily that he left behind his wallet and briefcase.

One such action sounded a bizarre note. On December 23, Lieutenant Colonel Lynn Moore, a battalion commander of the 82d Airborne, took off in an OH-58 scout helicopter to visit D Company, posted near the Canal. As he was observing his troops from above, three special-operations Black Hawks suddenly appeared and forced his pilot to land. When Moore's ship touched down, a fourth Black Hawk landed alongside and a squad of Delta Force commandos sprang out, weapons at the ready.

On hand for this display were members of D Company. "All they saw was these guys in Ninja outfits that had their battalion commander at bay," said Moore. The troopers cracked off a couple of warning shots, one of which ricocheted off the helicopter's instrument panel and zinged past Moore's head. At that point, the colonel leaped out and yelled to his men to cease fire. That put an end to the episode, which had begun when the commandos, in their zeal to capture Noriega—whom Moore himself had reported in the area—suspected the officer's flight of being an escape attempt in a purloined helicopter.

By this time, Noriega had taken to driving around in a blue Land Rover with tinted windows, changing locations every four hours. However, there were fewer and fewer places to hide. Finally, on Christmas Eve, Panama's erstwhile strongman ordered his driver to stop at a Dairy Queen ice cream store near Paitilla. There, Noriega telephoned Monsignor José Laboa, the papal ambassador to Panama, and pleaded for political asylum at the Vatican Embassy. At first, Laboa denied sanctuary, but as the dictator began to sound increasingly desperate, the ambassador agreed to send a driver to pick him up. At the same time, hoping that Noriega might yet be intercepted, Laboa telephoned Major General Marc Cisneros, commander of U.S. Army South, to tell him where Noriega could be found, but Cisneros could not take the call—and thus lost perhaps the best chance to collar the dictator.

A task force consisting of Delta Force operators and regular infantry had sealed off the Cuban and Nicaraguan embassies but, never dreaming that the dictator—not a follower of the Pope—would seek refuge at the papal mission, they had left it wide open. Noriega arrived wearing running shorts and a T-shirt and

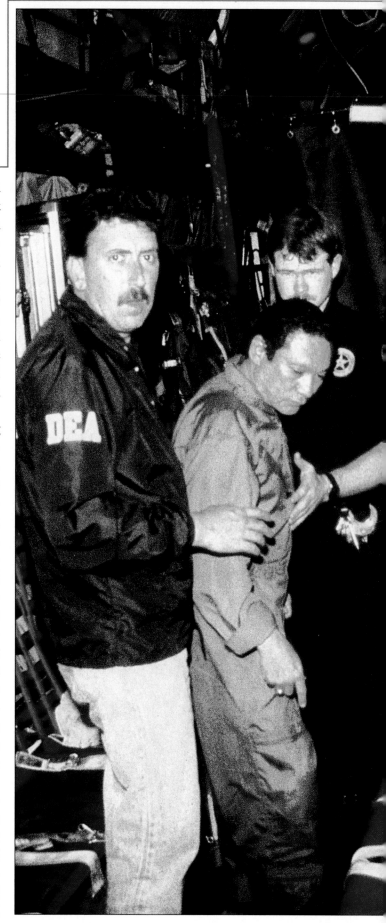

armed with two AK-47s, of which he was speedily relieved. "He looked like a hunted fox," said a witness.

A veritable storm of diplomatic and psychological activity ensued. U.S. State Department officials sought to convince the Vatican that Noriega was a common criminal and neither eligible for nor deserving of political asylum. American tanks, light armored vehicles, and hundreds of troops in combat gear ringed the Vatican mission. Helicopters buzzed loudly overhead, and a Spectre gunship orbited the area as a warning to any Noriega loyalists who might be contemplating a rescue. The Special Operation Command's Fourth Psyop Group arrived on the scene and commenced a campaign to unnerve Noriega. Day and night, loudspeakers assaulted the opera-loving fugitive with a cacophony of heavy rock, including such pointed numbers as "No Place To Run" and "You're No Good"—"the fingernails on the blackboard," said one officer.

Meanwhile, Monsignor Laboa had his own psychological strategy. He confined the dictator to a spartan room with opaqued windows and a broken TV set; he shut off the air conditioning and forbade alcoholic drinks. An embassy spokesman said the dictator looked "tired, pale, and depressed. He hardly speaks." Noriega was permitted to receive only one telephone call. It came from his long-time mistress, Vicky Amado, being held in U.S. custody. "Don't blow your brains out," she counseled. "Come out with dignity."

By New Year's Eve, Laboa received what he needed—a letter from Pope John Paul II branding Noriega a criminal ineligible for political asylum. At last, on January 3, 1990, at 8:50 p.m., the ex-dictator quietly walked to the gate of the embassy and turned himself over to U.S. authorities. He wore one of his general's uniforms someone had brought, and he carried a Bible Laboa had given him.

Less than an hour later, an Air Force MC-130 took off from Howard Air Force Base en route to Miami. Inside huddled the subdued little man who had once terrorized his nation. Upon arrival in Florida, he became federal prisoner 41586, charged with multiple counts of drug dealing and facing perhaps years in jail awaiting trial even if never convicted. Behind him, in Panama, lay an economy in ruins, hundreds of dead civilians and PDF troops, and hundreds more wounded. Altogether, 23 American troops—11 of whom were from special-operations units—had died to liberate Panama from his yoke, and 324, including 93 from the Special Operations Command, had been wounded. ★

Acknowledgments

The editors of Time-Life Books wish to thank the following for their assistance: Guy Aceto, *Air Force* magazine, Arlington, Va.; Major Mark Adkin, Bedford, England; Major Craig Barta, Fort Bragg, N.C.; Lieutenant Colonel Doug Brown, Fort Campbell, Ky.; C. A. Buxo, St. George's, Grenada, West Indies; Colonel John Collins (Ret.), Library of Congress, Washington, D.C.; Dorothy Cross, Pentagon, Washington, D.C.; David Deal, Magellan Systems Inc., Monrovia, Calif.; Mavis T. DeZulovich, Fort Belvoir, Va.; Lorna Dodt, Pentagon, Washington, D.C.; Colonel John W. Dye III, USSOCOM, MacDill Air Force Base, Fla.; Joe Gaylord, St. George's, Grenada, West Indies; George Grimes, USSOCOM, MacDill Air Force Base, Fla.; Major Kevin Higgins and the men of Seventh Special Forces Group (Airborne), Fort Bragg, N.C.; Peter A. Hnatiuk, Fort Bragg, N.C.; Laurel N. Holder, ITT, Roanoke, Va.; Hugh Howard, Pentagon, Washington, D.C.; David C. Isby, Alexandria, Va.; Kenneth G. Jensen, McDonnell Douglas Helicopter Co., Mesa, Ariz.; Ben Jones, Department of Defense, Washington, D.C.; Colonel William Kernan and the men of the 75th Ranger Regiment, Fort Benning, Ga.; Jack Kingston, Arlington, Va.; Hal Klopper, McDonnell Douglas Helicopter Co., Mesa, Ariz.; General James Lindsay (Ret.), Vass, N.C.; Irene Miner, Pentagon, Washington, D.C.; Lyle Minter, Pentagon, Washington, D.C.; Steve Moore, Fort Bragg, N.C.; Kurt F. Muse, Burke, Va.; Colonel Rod Paschall, Carlisle, Pa.; Commander Robert S. Pritchard, Naval Special Warfare Command, Coronado, Calif.; William Rosenmund, Pentagon, Washington, D.C.; William Salisbury, Bonita, Calif.; Lieutenant Colonel Dick Sheffield, USSOCOM, MacDill Air Force Base, Fla.; David Silbergeld, Nite Optics, Wilkes-Barre, Pa.; Mabel Thomas, Pentagon, Washington, D.C.

Bibliography

BOOKS

Adams, James, *Secret Armies: Inside the American, Soviet and European Special Forces.* New York: The Atlantic Monthly Press, 1988.

Adkin, Mark, *Urgent Fury: The Battle for Grenada* (Issues in Low-Intensity Conflict series). Lexington, Mass.: Lexington Books, 1989.

Bishop, Patrick, and John Witherow, *The Winter War: The Falklands.* New York: Quartet Books, 1982.

Burrowes, Reynold A., *Revolution and Rescue in Grenada: An Account of the U.S.-Caribbean Invasion.* New York: Greenwood Press, 1988.

Donnelly, Thomas, Margaret Roth, and Caleb Baker, *Just Cause: The Storming of Panama.* New York: Macmillan, Inc., 1991.

Eshel, David, *Elite Fighting Units.* New York: Arco Publishing, Inc., 1984.

Geraghty, Tony:
Inside the SAS. New York: Ballantine Books, 1980.
This is the SAS: A Pictorial History of the Special Air Service Regiment. New York: Arco Publishing, Inc., 1983.

Gunston, Bill, and Mike Spick, *Modern Fighting Helicopters: Full Details of the Aircraft, Their Weapons Systems and the Combat Tactics.* London: Salamander Books Ltd., 1986.

Hastings, Max, and Simon Jenkins, *The Battle for the Falklands.* New York: W. W. Norton & Company, 1983.

Isby, David C., *Weapons and Tactics of the Soviet Army.* New York: Jane's Publishing Inc., 1988.

Jane's Fighting Ships 1990-91, edited by Captain Richard Sharpe. Alexandria, Va.: Jane's Information Group Inc., 1990.

Ladd, James, *SBS—The Invisible Raiders: The History of the Special Boat Squadron from World War Two to the Present.* Devon, England: Davis & Charles Publishers, 1989.

Macdonald, Peter, *The SAS in Action.* London: Sidgwick & Jackson Limited, 1990.

McManners, Captain Hugh, *Falklands Commando.* London: Collins Publishing Group, 1987.

Markham, George, *Guns of the Elite.* Dorset, England: Arms and Armour Press, Ltd., 1987.

Middlebrook, Martin, *Task Force: The Falklands War, 1982.* New York: Viking Penguin, Inc., 1987.

The New Illustrated Science and Invention Encyclopedia. Westport, Conn.: H. S. Stuttman Inc. Publishers, 1987.

Perkins, Roger, *Operation Paraquat: The Battle for South Georgia.* Beckington, Somerset, England: Picton Publishing (Chippenham) Ltd., 1986.

Thompson, Julian, *No Picnic: 3 Commando Brigade in the South Atlantic: 1982.* New York: Hippocrene Books, 1985.

Welham, Michael, *Combat Frogmen: Military Diving from the Nineteenth Century to the Present Day.* Wellingborough, Northamptonshire, England: Patrick Stephens Limited, 1989.

PERIODICALS

"America's Secret Soldiers: The Buildup of U.S. Special Operations Forces." *The Defense Monitor*, June 4, 1985.

"The Battle for Grenada." *Newsweek*, November 7, 1983.

Blank, Richard W., "The NAVSTAR Global Positioning System." *Signal*, November 1986.

Capaccio, Tony:
"Task Force 160: The Army's High-Technology 'Night Stalkers.' " *Defense Electronics*, November 1989.
"U.S. Commandos Fly Silent Choppers." *Defense Week* (Washington, D.C.), February 22, 1988.

Christy, John, "The Diverse Defender." *International Combat Arms*, January 1987.

"D-Day in Grenada." *Time*, November 7, 1983.

"Debacle in the Desert." *Time*, May 5, 1980.

DeZulovich, Mavis, "Image Intensification Technology." *Army Research, Development & Acquisition Bulletin*, May-June 1988.

Donnelly, Tom, "Don't Underestimate the U.S. Army." *Washington Post*, January 6, 1990.

Emerson, Steven, "What Went Wrong on Grenada?" *U.S. News & World Report*, November 3, 1986.

Fialka, John J., "In Battle for Grenada, Commando Missions Didn't Go as Planned." *Wall Street Journal*, November 15, 1983.

Henderson, Breck W., "Ground Forces Rely on GPS to Navigate Desert Terrain." *Aviation Week & Space Technology*, February 11, 1991.

Hughes, David, "Night Invasion of Panama Required Special Operations Aircraft, Training." *Aviation Week & Space Technology*, February 19, 1990.

"Hughes/Racal 530MG: High Tech for the Light Attack Helicopter." *Rotor & Wing International*, May 1985.

Livingstone, Neil C.:
"Danger in the Air." *The Washingtonian*, June 1990.
"Just Cause Jailbreak: U.S. Delta Force Rescues American in Panama." *Soldier of Fortune*, November 1990.

Luttwak, Edward N., "In Grenada." *Harper's Magazine*, March 1985.

"McDonnell Douglas—Aircraft: USA." *Jane's All the World's Aircraft, 1987-1988*. New York: Jane's Publishing Co., 1988.

"McDonnell Douglas—Aircraft: USA." *Jane's All the World's Aircraft, 1990*. New York: Jane's Publishing Co., 1990.

Magnuson, Ed, "Caught in the Act." *Time*, October 5, 1987.

Marsh, George, "GPS Sets Course." *Space* (Burnham, Buckinghamshire, England), November-December, 1990.

Miller, Barry, "GPS Proves Its Worth in Operation Desert Storm." *Armed Forces Journal International*, April 1991.

Nordwall, Bruce D., "ITT Solves Complex Problems to Produce Image Intensifiers." *Aviation Week & Space Technology*, May 22, 1989.

Salisbury, Bill:
"Operation Screw Up." *New Times* (Miami, Fla.), November 7-13, 1990.
"War Beneath the Waves." *San Diego Weekly*, October 4, 1990.

Seibert, Sam, "The 'Night Stalkers': Death in the Dark." *Newsweek*, October 5, 1987.

Simpson, Ross, "Devil in Disguise." *Soldier of Fortune*, May 1990.

Smith, William E., "Running the Gauntlet." *Time*, August 3, 1987.

"Stealth Fighter Pilots Insist They Didn't Miss in Panama." *Air Force Times*, June 10, 1991.

" 'Surgical Firepower' Trashed Noriega Post." *Washington Times*, January 11, 1990.

"Task Force 160: The Night Stalkers." *Defence Update International*, 1985.

Trewhitt, Henry, "Coping with Khomeini." *U.S. News & World Report*, August 3, 1987.

"U.S., Caribbean States Invade Grenada; Cuban Resistance Stronger Than Expected." *Facts on File*, October 28, 1983.

"U.S. Attacks, Seizes Iranian Mine Ship." *Facts on File*, September 25, 1987.

Walker, Greg, "Eyes in the Dark: Night Vision in a New Light." *International Combat Arms*, July 1989.

Watson, Russell, "A U.S. Ambush in the Gulf." *Newsweek*, October 5, 1987.

OTHER

Adcock, Gene, "Night Vision Equipment: A Planners Guide." Booklet. Tempe, Ariz.: Litton Electron Devices Division, Night Vision Department, 1990.

After-Action Report from Seventh Special Forces Group. Fort Bragg, N.C.: Department of the Army, January 27, 1990.

Akers, Colonel Frank, "Operation Just Cause: The Warriors." Booklet. 1990.

"The C³I Handbook: Edition Three: Command, Control, Communications, Intelligence." Handbook. Prepared by the editors of *Defense Electronics*. Palo Alto, Calif.: EW Communications, Inc., 1988.

Collins, John, "United States and Soviet Special Operations." Study by the Congressional Research Service, Library of Congress, prepared at the request of the Special Operations Panel of the Committee on Armed Services, House of Representatives, 100th Congress. Washington, D.C.: U.S. Government Printing Office, April 28, 1987.

"FM 21-26: Map Reading and Land Navigation." Manual. Washington, D.C.: U.S. Department of the Army, September 1987.

"Memorandum for RS5." After-Action Report from 75th Ranger Regiment. Fort Benning, Ga.: Department of the Army, December 6, 1990.

"Operation Just Cause: Rangers at Rio Hato." Print of After-Action Slide Show from 1990, compiled by 75th Ranger Regiment. Fort Benning, Ga.: Department of the Army, 1990.

"Securing the Pacora River Bridge, 20 December 1989." After-Action Report from Seventh Special Forces Group. Fort Bragg, N.C.: Department of the Army, 1990.

Stiner, Lieutenant General Carl W., "Joint Task Force South in Operation Just Cause: 20 December 1989-12 January 1990." Oral History Interviews with Dr. Robert K. Wright, Jr. Fort Bragg, N.C.: Department of the Army, March, June 1990.

"Subskimmer." Booklet. Hexham, Northumberland, England: Defence Boats Ltd. No date.

Index

Picture Credits

The sources for the illustrations that appear in this book are listed below. Credits from left to right are separated by semicolons; from top to bottom they are separated by dashes.
Cover: William B. Folsom/Arms Communications. 6, 7: Department of Defense/U.S. Air Force (2)—Phil Prater/*Soldiers* magazine. 8, 9: Department of Defense/U.S. Air Force; Department of Defense—Rick Mullen/Foto Consortium; Department of Defense—Department of Defense/U.S. Air Force. 10, 11: Mike Nelson/Agence France Presse, Paris—D. Hudson/Sygma; P. Durand/Sygma. 12: U.S. Navy, (DN-SC-87-12580). 14, 15: U.S. Army. 17: U.S. Navy, (DN-SC-87-12584). 18, 19: U.S. Navy, (DN-
SC-87-12588); (DN-SN-88-09568). 21: Private collection. 22, 23: Art by Kim Barnes of Stansbury, Ronsaville, Wood, Inc., photo from private collection. 24-27: Private collection. 28: Wollmann/Gamma, Paris. 31: Map by Mapping Specialists Ltd. 35: Defence Boats Ltd., Hexham, Northumberland. 36, 37: Defence Boats Ltd., Hexham, Northumberland (4); art by Fred Holz (4). 40, 41: Press Association, London; Crown Copyright. 45: Press Association, London. 50, 51: Paul Haley/*Soldier* magazine, Aldershot, Hants. 52, 53: Hugh McManners, Petham, Kent. 56, 57: Hugh McManners, Petham, Kent (2). 58, 59: Paul Haley/*Soldier* magazine, Aldershot, Hants. 60, 61: Hugh McManners, Petham, Kent. 62: Department of

Defense, (DD-ST-84-08783). 64: Map by Mapping Specialists Ltd. 66: C. A. Buxo, St. George's, Grenada. 69: Brice Vican. 72, 73: Courtesy Mark Adkin, Bedford, Bedfordshire; U.S. Air Force (2). 77: Art by Mark Seidler. 78, 79: Department of Defense. 81: Mark Adkin, Bedford, Bedfordshire. 82, 83: Johnson/Woodfin Camp; Mark Adkin, Bedford, Bedfordshire. 84, 85: C. T. U., Inc. 86, 87: Courtesy Mark Adkin, Bedford, Bedfordshire. 90, 91: Jean-Louis Atlan/Sygma. 94, 95: Mark Adkin, Bedford, Bedfordshire (4). 96, 97: C. A. Buxo, St. George's, Grenada. 98, 99: Art by Mark Robinson (2); Mark Meyer. 100, 101: Art by Mark Robinson. 102, 103: Satchel charge art and line charge art by Mark Robinson—art by Mike Mikos. 104-105: Art by Mark Robinson; art by Mike Mikos (2). 106, 107: Art by Mark Robinson; art by Mike Mikos (2). 108, 109: Art by Mark Robinson; art by Mike Mikos (3). 110: U.S. Air Force. 114: *La Republica*, Panama. 117: Map by Mapping Specialists Ltd. 119: Mark Meyer. 120: Art by Steven R. Wagner. 121: Mark Meyer (5). 124, 125: Art by Lloyd K. Townsend. 129: Courtesy James B. Zazas (2)—Stuart Warner—Department of Defense. 130, 131: U.S. Air Force/Technical Sergeant H. H. Deffner. 132: U.S. Army. 134: Department of Defense (2)—Kevin Jenkins and Stuart Warner. 138, 139: Courtesy Kurt Frederick Muse. 140, 141: Courtesy Kurt Frederick Muse, copied by Renée Comet. 143: Magellan Systems Corporation. 144, 145: Art by Lloyd K. Townsend. 147: U.S. Army. 148, 149: Ronald Drucker. 150, 151: Christopher Morris/Black Star. 152, 153: Department of Defense, courtesy Robert F. Dorr.

Time-Life Books
is a division of Time Life Inc.,
a wholly owned subsidiary of
THE TIME INC. BOOK COMPANY

TIME-LIFE BOOKS

MANAGING EDITOR: Thomas H. Flaherty
Director of Editorial Resources: Elise D. Ritter-Clough
Director of Photography and Research:
John Conrad Weiser
Editorial Board: Dale M. Brown, Roberta Conlan, Laura Foreman, Lee Hassig, Jim Hicks, Blaine Marshall, Rita Thievon Mullin, Henry Woodhead

Associate Publisher: Ann M. Mirabito
Editorial Director: Russell B. Adams, Jr.
Marketing Director: Anne C. Everhart
Production Manager: Prudence G. Harris
Supervisor of Quality Control: James King

Editorial Operations
Production: Celia Beattie
Library: Louise D. Forstall
Computer Composition: Deborah G. Tait (Manager), Monika D. Thayer, Janet Barnes Syring, Lillian Daniels

Correspondents: Elisabeth Kraemer-Singh (Bonn); Christine Hinze (London); Christina Lieberman (New York); Maria Vincenza Aloisi (Paris); Ann Natanson (Rome). Valuable assistance was also provided by Marlin Levin and Jean Max (Jerusalem), Elizabeth Brown and Katheryn White (New York), John Maier (Rio de Janiero), Ulric Mentus (Trinidad).

THE NEW FACE OF WAR

SERIES EDITOR: Lee Hassig
Series Administrator: Judith W. Shanks

Editorial Staff for *Commando Operations*
Art Directors: Christopher M. Register, Fatima Taylor
Picture Editor: Marion Ferguson Briggs
Text Editors: Charlotte Anker, Stephen G. Hyslop, Paul Mathless
Senior Writer: James M. Lynch
Associate Editors/Research: Robin Currie, Mark Lazen
Writer: Charles J. Hagner
Assistant Editors/Research: Jennifer L. Pearce, Mark Rogers
Assistant Art Director: Sue Ellen Pratt
Senior Copy Coordinators: Anthony K. Pordes (principal), Elizabeth Graham
Picture Coordinator: David Beard
Editorial Assistant: Kathleen S. Walton

Special Contributors: Champ Clark, George Daniels, John DeMott, Edward Edelson, Lee Ewing, Craig Roberts, Charles W. Sasser, Edward Stafford, Diane Ullius (text); Doug Brown, Katya Sharpe Cooke, Clay Griffith, Ellen Gross, Catherine Halesky, Lawrence Helm, Christine Soares, Susan Sonnesyn, Marie Tessier (research); Mel Ingber (index).

Library of Congress Cataloging in Publication Data
Commando operations/by the editors of Time-Life Books.
    p.   cm.   (The New face of war).
    Includes bibliographical references and index.
    ISBN 0-8094-8616-4
    1. Commando troops. 2. Special forces (Military science).
I. Time-Life Books. II. Series.
U262.C653 1991
356'.167—dc20   90-27511 CIP
ISBN 0-8094-8617-2 (lib. bdg.)